REAL LIFE 101

MW01697823

REAL LIFE 101

The Graduate's Guide to Survival

Susan Kleinman

MasterMedia Limited
New York

For My Parents, Eunice and Bernie,
Who Prepared Me for Real Life

Copyright © 1989, 1992 by Susan Kleinman
All rights reserved
including the right of reproduction
in whole or in part in any form.
Published by MasterMedia Limited

MASTERMEDIA and colophon are registered
trademarks of MasterMedia Limited
Designed by Al Cetta
Manufactured in the United States of America
10 9 8 7 6 5 4 3 2 1

Library of Congress Cataloging-in-Publication Data

Kleinman, Susan, 1964-
Real life 101.

1. Life skills—United States. 2. College
graduates—United States—Life skills guides.
I. Title. II. Title: Real life one hundred one.
III. Title: Real life one hundred and one.
HQ2039.U6K54 1988 305′.9069 88-27345
ISBN 0-942361-44-X

Contents

REAL LIFE 101

Introduction

Real Life, Here We Come

When my friends and I graduated college in 1986, the world was our oyster. In fact, it was our Oyster Rockefeller. The job market—and the stock market—was booming, and art-history majors who couldn't balance their checkbooks were able to land $50,000-a-year jobs on Wall Street. Engineers were in higher demand than ever before, and even those of us who sought careers in the "artistic" fields didn't have to live like starving artists.

The mood was as buoyant as the economy: America was enjoying peace and prosperity, and those who had signed up for ROTC to pay for college were certain that the toughest duty they'd ever pull was KP at a stateside army base. AIDS was something we were sure would happen only to *other* people—and *other* people's friends—and those who wished to turn a blind eye to the growing problem of homelessness and poverty could do so merely by taking a different route to work.

But a lot has changed since then. The economy has taken a nose dive and the numbers of ill and homeless have climbed skyward. Since the first edition of *Real Life 101* was published in 1989, we have all watched the Berlin Wall tumble and the social-service system crumble. In the past year alone, the Cold War has given way to the Gulf War, and Americans have given their lives in the first war any of us born post-1965 can remember with any clarity.

But it's not just the world that's changed; *we're* changing, too. Young Americans are returning to the social consciousness that has been long dormant on the American scene. We're worried about the less fortunate, and we're well aware that even the *more* fortunate among us are likely to be less well-off than our parents were. We're saying "no" to twenty-four-hour-a-day jobs and "yes" when charitable organizations call and ask us to give of our time and of ourselves.

And, today's college graduate has a great deal in common with those who donned caps and gowns in 1986—and in 1976, for that matter. You, too, are worried about finding a job you can like and a mate you can love. You're trying to make new friends and keep the old, as Grandma advised, and looking for affordable ways to spend your time with those friends. You're worried about staying healthy and sane, and, perhaps most of all, you wonder what Real Life has in store for you.

I know just how you feel: in the spring of 1986, as my graduation from the University of Pennsylvania drew nearer, strains of "Pomp and Circumstance" began playing in my head like the shark-warning music in *Jaws*. In mid-April, my hysteria advanced from a dull throb to a full-throttle panic attack when I spotted a damp piece of mail wedged in the box between my final-notice phone bill and a flier for an overnight thesis-typing service. Lying there in a word-processor-addressed envelope (a *thin* envelope) was my fifty-seventh job-rejection letter.

"Thank you for your interest in Hendricks, Shmendricks, and Lye," it read. "We regret to inform you that we have no openings suitable for someone with your experience."

I would never find a job, I cried to myself every night for a week. I would never make it in the real world. I longed to be a freshman again. I pined for the days when my biggest dilemma was whether to buy the blue knapsack or the red. I yearned for the days when my worst fear was getting caught stealing silverware from the university dining service.

I quickly realized, though, that I could circumvent the difficulties of life after graduation by simply failing to graduate. Indeed, this possibility loomed more likely as my attentions shifted earlier and earlier each weeknight from John Dos Passos to more than one Dos Equis. Though I wasn't taking "Literature of the Depression" for a grade, I was well aware that an eighth-semester course is never taken pass/fail, but pass/don't graduate. And what if I *didn't?* Anxiety abounded.

Soon enough, panic over the prospect of being stuck in college my whole life was replaced by realization of the sad truth: I couldn't stick myself on campus forever, even if I wanted to. The question, therefore, wasn't "What if I don't graduate and get a job?" but "WHAT IF I DO?!" (And, of course, I would.) I was looking forward to graduation and employment with as much glee as I anticipate a trip to the dentist. But unlike my teeth-drilling appointments, which

I have successfully avoided for three years running, graduation and employment came right on schedule.

On the 102-degree day I graduated from Penn, one of my classmates hung a banner from the football bleachers where our proud and relieved parents sat. "Real Life," read the painted bedsheet, "here we come!"

And there we went. One day, we're all students. Young, striving minds with common pursuits: a gut course and a date for Saturday night. Turn around and we're all searching for something else: an excuse to stay in college four more years.

No such luck.

The phone call I received the morning after graduation was not, despite my prayers, the college registrar phoning to revoke my diploma and re-enroll me for four years of expensive textbooks and cheap beer. Rather, the voice on the other end issued an invitation to participate in the public relations training program in New York to which I had applied in March. Deciding that the only thing worse than having to go to a job was having to *look* for one, I grabbed the offer. Thus was I matriculated into Real Life 101, that can't-place-out-of-it-even-with-AP-credit course requirement for a major in the real world.

In this particular "seminar," I quickly learned, there were to be few multiple choice tests. No incompletes would be granted. More frightening still, participation would count for more than the collegiate 10 percent of my grade. It soon became clear, too, that in Real Life, no one takes notes for you when you're out. There are "finals" every day of your working life. Worst of all, there are NO Cliff Notes.

This book, then, is my best shot at lending you my notes. In compiling them, I have drawn on the advice of some "teaching assistants" (all English-speaking, for a change) —professionals in various fields who have offered to share their tips on how to make it on a starting salary . . . how to make the most of your first job . . . how to find a new home and make it your own . . . how to keep your body and your mind in smooth working order . . . and where to go for help when you need it.

To make sure that I wasn't the only one experiencing the postgrad crazies, I surveyed recent graduates from all over the United States. Friends and strangers from across the country completed a four-page questionnaire on topics ranging from money to love. "What was the best thing to happen to you since graduation?" I asked. "What was the worst?"

Most recent graduates agreed that the best part about Real Life is, as one woman wrote, "It's my life! No matter how hard I have to work, when I come home at night, work is over, and it's not hanging over my head like a midterm. And as much as I miss living in a dorm, it's nice not to have people looking over my shoulder, watching me. I can be what I want, and do what I want. Sometimes, that makes me nervous, but most of the time I love it."

Still, most of us feel nostalgic for college. Among the things people miss most are:

"Walking into a bar and knowing everyone inside. Even if I went in alone, I had a blast."

"I miss having the time to do whatever."

"The academic environment."

"Poetry classes."

"Having no responsibilities."

The list goes on, and many say that what they miss most is "MY FRIENDS!!" Surely the hardest part of graduating and starting a job is the loss of that twenty-four-hour party. It will never again be as easy to make friends or to find time to spend with them.

But now for the good news. Never again will you have to

wake up at 7:00 on Saturday morning to pull on dirty sweatpants and stumble to the library to study organic chemistry. Never will you stay up through the night writing a fifty-page paper you started yesterday. No one will ever ask you the dates of the Malta and Yalta conferences. I promise.

Here are some of the other things the graduates I spoke with were happy to kiss good-bye:

"Freshmen. First I hated being one, then I hated dealing with them."

"The group mentality."

"The surprise quiz I was never ready for."

"Eight-thirty classes."

"Cramming for exams."

"Multiple choice tests."

"Having to hit my parents up for money to buy textbooks I knew I would never open."

In the course of the interviews I conducted, I heard over and over again that the transition to Real Life is a difficult one—but one that can be mastered. I discovered that there are no right or wrong ways to make the adjustment—but there are *better* ways. And I found out that people were eager to share their stories.

I read dozens of funny "worst date stories" and riotous adventures in apartment hunting. There were sad stories, too. Many of us have lost people we love since graduation. Some have seen their parents split up after thirty-year marriages. And others have seen their own romances fade . . . or explode.

But I read about plenty of triumphs, as well. Some of the graduates who helped me with my research had moved clear across the country and discovered that they could make it on their own. Others found professional successes, unexpected love, and the joy that comes with tackling the challenges that Real Life likes to throw our way.

Some of the experiences I've presented in *Real Life 101* were shared by everyone I spoke with, whether they graduated from a small college in 1983 or a huge law school in '91. For example, almost no one saves any money, regardless of salary. Everyone wants to be in love. Many of us live on pasta. And most of us have noticed that, to paraphrase Mark Twain, the older we grow, the smarter our parents get.

Other insights and stories I heard were as unique as the special people who shared them with me. And some of the stories are my own. On the clichéd theory that my life would have been easier "if I had known then what I know now," I have shared some of my own adventures during that first year: the year I survived my first job, first blind date, and first business trip. The year I learned that there *is* life after college, but *not* after midnight. Not when I have an 8:00 A.M. staff meeting the next day.

Real Life 101 is, in a sense, an edited diary of my first year. Make that my first year-or-so. Your "first year" won't last 365 days. It may take eight months and fourteen minutes, or fourteen months and eight days. Your "first year" will be more a state of mind than a matter of time. You'll know you've made it through when you realize that you almost *like* working, and have stopped spending your weeks wondering what you'd be doing "at this very second" if you were still on campus. That scary transition is over when you've accepted the fact that you'll never again have four months a year off, and when you have not only committed—but overcome—at least one real-life blunder of tearjerking proportions.

It's over, most of all, when you realize that you not only *can* survive the transition to Real Life, but you *have*. And more than survived—you've succeeded.

Good luck!!

1

A Hunting You Will Go . . .

Finding a Job When the Job Market's Crunched

If you've landed a job before graduation, consider yourself lucky. In the 1980s, when corporate recruiters swarmed college campuses like ants at a picnic, it was quite common for seniors to have their job plans secure before they were even sure where they'd be spending spring break. Today, though, companies are cutting back on expensive recruiting, waiting instead for applicants to approach them, and many companies have started limiting their hiring.

With these factors working against you, you'll have to take a strategic approach to job hunting, and the search may be longer and tougher than you'd like. There's good news, though, too: even many companies that *are* laying off continue to hire entry-level workers. Why? Simple: They can pay you less for the same work. Also, while some fields have dried up or shrunk, new areas of opportunity are opening all the time. The biggest of these is the chance to work at a fledgling, entrepreneurial venture. These aren't the companies that advertise in the want ads; they're the ones you hear about through the grapevine. They aren't the big-name companies, they're the big-opportunity companies. My friend Amy, who worked for a start-up company even before the start-up trend started, has this to say about her experiences:

"I got to do much more, so much sooner than I would have at a big company. Just a few months after I started, I was one of seven people who made a presentation to a group of important London bankers who came to meet with us. I never would have gotten to do that in a big company."

A smaller company isn't likely to come hunting for *you*, though; you've got to do some research to find them. Here are a few good ways to start:

- Ask around. It seems everyone knows *someone* these days who's leaving the corporate world to hang out a private shingle. Because they, themselves, are used to relying on the "kindness of strangers," and because they often have less rigid mind-sets (and schedules!), entrepreneurs are often willing to sit down with young job hunters and chat. Even if your initial contact has no openings for you, she is likely to know several other new-business owners. Experts at the outplacement counseling firm Challenger, Gray and Christmas in Chicago estimate that 40 percent of all jobs are landed through personal contacts. You don't have to be "well connected" in the old-money/old-school-ties sense, either. Everyone knows *somebody* who has just opened up a business, and among all your friends and relatives and *their* acquaintances, you're sure to amass several dozen prospects.

- Magazines such as *Entrepreneur* and *Working Woman*—as well as many regional and local papers—often run feature stories about men and women who are starting their own companies. Spend some time in the library; you're likely to come up with a list of names. Send a letter referencing the article and the reasons you'd like to work for the company along with your résumé, and follow up with a phone call.
- Your college's alumni magazine probably has listings of which graduates are doing what. Scan back issues for alumni notes or talk directly to the alumni relations office; they may be able to steer you toward alumni who have young companies.

Once you do locate a small company you want to work for, your access to it should be easier, says James Challenger, president of Challenger, Gray and Christmas, because you don't have as many layers of management to go through. The decision-making is liable to be quicker too, says Challenger, because not as many people are involved in it.

In addition to broadening your search to include smaller companies, you may have to re-evaluate what kind of job you're willing to take. While many fields are shrinking, and many offices have a freeze on hiring, there are still plenty of growth areas. Not surprisingly, debt and bankruptcy counseling is a growing field, as is anything connected to stress alleviation.

But even if you're trained in one of these fields (or have applicable education) the job isn't going to leap out of the sidewalk and grab you by the throat. If you have skills that aren't marketable in the corporate sector, consider working in a government agency. The SEC, the IRS, and the Justice Department all pay less than private enterprises, but they offer excellent opportunities and the chance to make contacts that will serve you well when you *do* cross over into the profit-making sector.

Whatever kind of job you're hunting for, the hardest part about job hunting is getting started. "For six months," one mother told me, "my son was résumé paralyzed. Colleges don't teach our children how to look for jobs; kids are used to being taken care of by their parents, and when they get out, they don't know what to do first." What did *her* kids do first? One scooped ice cream for half a year, and one tended lobsters in a pound. When they were ready to start looking and accept the fact that they were on their own, they were both able to find good jobs.

The ice cream–scooping route may not be as glamorous as an instant jump to CEO, but it has its advantages: a low-pressure job will give you time to think about what you want to do and will give you a source of income while you are hunting for your "real" job. If you can't stand the sight of chocolate chips, there are plenty of other things you can do to fill the gap between the classroom and the corporate conference room:

- Babysit. In big cities, nannies get about $350 a week off the books. (Not that we're encouraging you to cheat on your taxes, mind you, but sometimes, people, . . . well, they just forget to fill out those pesky forms.)
- Tutor high school students. Tutors can make over $20 an hour, and since most tutoring is done in the late afternoon, you'll have plenty of time during the day to set up job interviews. SAT-prep courses like Stanley Kaplan and Princeton Review are always on the lookout for classroom instructors. Since many young professionals moonlight as test-prep coaches, you're likely

to meet people who are working in the field you're interested in.

- Teach aerobics. In many gyms, you need to be licensed, but once you are, you can pick up money while you stay in shape and meet lots of overstressed career types who may just know of corporate job openings. If you don't know a leotard from a ligament, you can lifeguard for a health club pool (if you are licensed), or tend the locker room of a gym. Many clubs will give you free membership in exchange.
- Teach, period. Teachers for America sends non-education majors to teach in underprivileged areas, as a way of improving the school systems. Graduates who've done it say the experience has improved *their* lives immeasurably, too. The program requires a two-year commitment—but who knows? By then, the recession may be over!
- Work as a freelance fact-checker. Lots of magazines hire part-timers to double-check writers' accuracy. (Remember *Bright Lights, Big City?*; the main character was a fact-checker). Besides keeping your intellect sharp, fact-checking is a great way to make contacts in the magazine business.
- Do office temp work. Night-shift typists can make $30 an hour, and day-shift workers have the chance to meet all the executives they're typing for.
- Tend bar or work in a hotel. Some of the interesting people you meet may have job leads; the others may leave big tips.
- Sell door-to-door. Companies like Avon offer the opportunity to hone your sales skills while you make money. Because you set your own hours, you can continue selling cosmetics to earn extra money even after

you've landed a full-time job. (You can call Avon at 800-858-8000 for more information.)

This last option and others that offer flexible hours are ideal for job-hunting times because they needn't interfere with your interviewing schedule. Remember that it can take up to a year to find a "real" job, particularly if you're interested in an obscure field or if you haven't yet clarified your goals in your own mind. Therefore, don't feel inadequate if you're still unemployed, even if all your friends already have work lined up. If all your hard work still leaves you jobless and dispirited, you may want to consider relocating to an area less hard hit by the recession. At the time of this writing, the Northwest was the most fertile job-hunting ground in the country.

The key is remaining flexible—and that means being willing to compromise not only about *where* you'll work, but about what you'll do. If you identify your target job too narrowly, you're likely to miss out on a golden (or at least silver-plated) opportunity in another realm. That's why these days, the ideal résumé starts off not with an "objective," but with a summary of your skills. (Let's face it: your objective may very well be to get a job. Period.) According to *Business Week* magazine, the old-style résumé—objective/education/experience—has been reshuffled so that your skills are listed first, your experience second, and your education last. While this may highlight the *lack* of experience any twenty-two-year-old has, it gives you the advantage of trumpeting skills you may have acquired in nonprofessional settings. Have you worked on the Multiple Sclerosis Dance-a-thon? You have special-events-organizing skills. Have you edited your fraternity's alumni newsletter? You've got editing experience to talk about—and to list in the "skills summary" at the top of your résumé. Volunteer work may not count as employment experience in the technical sense, but the skills it imparts can be a big boost in your job hunt.

So can a very active networking plan and a healthy dose of determination and stick-to-it-iveness. These days, more than ever, you have to be active in your job hunt. Follow up on letters, phone calls, and first interviews aggressively, and don't keep your focus too narrow. If you remain flexible and optimistic (who wants to hire a downer?), you *will* find a job. It may not be your dream job (few first jobs are), but it will allow you to start acquiring experience that will serve you well when you're ready for your *second* job, a few years down the line.

2

Hi Ho, Hi Ho, It's Off to Work We Go . . .

Getting Off to a Good Start at the Office

Once you have landed and celebrated your job, the reality sets in. . . . Now that you have a job, you've got to *do* it. This will probably necessitate awakening at an hour you haven't seen since you were being breast-fed. Unlike 9:00 classes, 9:00 punch-in times are nearly inescapable. And there's no back row to slink into if you show up late. Of course, the most important day to show up on time is the first.

Remember the first day of school? You had a new outfit, a new lunch box, and a new case of the weepies. "I DON'T WANT TO GO!!" you screamed as the school bus screeched to a halt in front of your house. "I'M NOT READY!!" The first day of work is all too similar, with a few minor adjustments. First, you probably had to pay for today's new outfit yourself, to the tune of a week's as-yet-unearned salary. Your "lunch box" is the briefcase you received for graduation in lieu of the Walkman you so pointedly hinted for. You're still NOT READY!! But the bus doesn't stop in front of your house. No way. By the time you've walked to the commuter train station or driven through rush hour traffic, you're ready for naptime. Remember naptime? Forget it.

Hopefully, that new outfit you paid for doesn't have a pinafore, or a picture of Mickey Mouse silk-screened on the rump. Neither should today's rising young executive carry a briefcase (or lunch box) bearing the likeness of any fictional character whose first name is "Super——."

So what *should* you wear? Weather permitting, you can wear what you wore for your interview. It impressed them once. . . . Otherwise, a basic suit/shirt/tie combo or, for women, a suit and blouse or a nice dress is appropriate to most office situations. Depending on your gender, you'll have to wear a necktie or pantyhose no matter how hot it is that first day. (That's another good reason not to care if you don't start work till next winter.)

Before you go out and invest in a whole new working wardrobe, analyze how your office mates and superiors clothe themselves. No sense investing in twenty-seven suits if skirts and casual sweaters are the office uniform. Neither will you want wild sports jackets if all the successful men in your company are pinstriped from head to toe.

A word of advice to those of you who are starting work before your graduation-week hangover even wears off: in evaluating the office dress code, don't assume that the wardrobes parading through the stifling hot hallways on July 1 are a good indication of the year-round fashion forecast. Many companies are more casual in the summertime than when the temperature drops. To avoid making expensive mistakes, wait till September to buy your fall clothes. This will also help you avoid paying preseason prices.

In fact, your best plan of attack is to spend a few weeks sizing up your workplace's unwritten dress code, and then shopping for your basic wardrobe at one time. This will save you both the traffic-hours of driving to a different mall every Saturday for one piece of clothing and the frustration of discovering that the black sweater you thought would look so perfect with your gray slacks actually looks funny with them. (Why does that always happen at ten-to-work-time the morning you were going to wear the outfit?)

According to Marcy Syms, president of Syms, which has stores along the East Coast and in the Midwest and Southwest, the best thing to bring to your shopping trip (besides legal tender, of course) is brand knowledge. Not surprising news from a woman who can be seen on TV explaining why an educated consumer is the best customer.

"The most important thing to look for," says Syms, "is value. Value in clothing is quality and styling at a low price. So, first, you have to know what clothes, and which manufacturers' merchandise, look good on you. What's made well? What does it cost at the department store? Once you know what you're looking for, value means finding it at the best price."

We're talking bargains here. Which doesn't necessarily mean cheap. Cheap falls apart at the seams. A bargain lasts. (Syms says you should expect three to five years' wear out of reasonably good clothes.) A bargain looks as if it cost more than it actually did.

But even when you're bargain-savvy, your funds are sure to be limited, unless your kind of "chic" is spelled "sheik" —preferably with an abundance of oil wells in the family. To make your money go further, build on a basic wardrobe and jazz it up with accessories.

For men, this means three basic suits, gray gabardine trousers and a navy blazer, enough white shirts to last until you get around to doing your laundry, and some terrific ties. (Depending on your industry, "terrific" can mean red silk with tiny paisleys, or it can mean an Italian-designer number with more colors than the oil spill under your car. Know your corporate culture before you shop.) Because most suits are variations on the basic theme (blue, gray, tan; chalk stripes, pinstripes, solids), the most important factors are fabric, quality, and fit. Marcy Syms warns against trying to alter a regular suit to your short body, or trying to get away with a snug European fit if your body has seen too many American apple pies. For most men, the best suit is a natural shoulder, with pleats, or not, at the waist, and no cuffs. And when it comes to fabric, "polyester has gotten a bad rap. Of course you don't want a suit that looks like polyester," says Syms, "but a little bit of it blended in to the fabric will make the suit last longer and wrinkle less, which means less dry cleaning." (In addition to eating away at your budget, dry cleaning also gnaws at the fibers of your clothes, shortening their life span.)

A woman with $500 to spend can put together a basic wardrobe, too, if she shops smart. Syms suggests a dress that's as simply styled as possible, a well-tailored skirt in a go-with-everything dark color like navy or black, trousers in the same color, a patterned blazer (plaids usually work well) that picks up the color of your "bottoms," and two blouses: one white, with a man-tailored or notched collar, and one in a pretty color, with a plain round ("jewel") collar, that can be accessorized to the max with costume jewelry and scarves. If you have some money left over (or want an incentive to save a little up), go for a sweater in red —or another shade that makes you look and feel wonderful.

"The Europeans have been dressing this way for years,"

says Syms. They have some basic pieces that will last for ages, and change the look with accessories, so that they stand out. Americans are finally learning to do this, too, and to use those finishing touches to keep themselves from fading into the woodwork or looking like everyone else.

"The only time you want to fade into the woodwork," Syms says, "is when you're afraid of getting fired; otherwise, you want to stand out . . . to be recognized. Looking professional is an important part of this. The negative impressions people get as a result of clothing are very subtle; your boss won't consciously realize that she doesn't trust your judgment because your seams are puckered; she'll just notice a vague feeling in the pit of her stomach that tells her you haven't impressed her.

"The micro skirt may look great on the weekend," says Syms, "but don't try it in the office Monday through Friday; it's not appropriate for the workplace."

Nor is the super-casual look: "Comfortable sneakers are fine when you're running for the bus," Syms says, "but be sure you change into one- or two-inch heeled pumps before having your morning coffee with the boss. If you work on your feet (in sales or making large-group presentations) look for the more comfortable pumps and ankle boots the manufacturers have started introducing. They have rubber soles for comfort and look good with skirts or tailored pants."

"Tailored" is the key word. "Personally, I love wearing slacks to work," says Syms. "I feel they allow me an ease of motion and flexibility that I don't have in pantyhose and a skirt. But you have to be careful not to wear slacks that make you look like you should be home painting your apartment."

And, while you want to fit in and look terrific, you don't

want to look like everybody else. To get a sense of what look you'll feel comfortable with, walk around the department stores that have clothes separated by designers. After you recover from the shock induced by the price tags, analyze your reactions: Did you gravitate toward designers who specialize in very tailored clothing, or flowing lines? Do you prefer an all-American look, or a more European cut?

On the subject of that American look, Marcy Syms offers a word of warning: the "classic" Shetland-sweater-and-jeans look isn't as go-everywhere as it seemed when you bought it. Forget about work (true of any jeans combo); even for your weekends, you should try to stick with a more unique look. Sure, jeans and a bulky sweater are "perfect" if you're in Connecticut at 3:00 P.M. on a Saturday afternoon. But they'll often make you (male or female) look like that sack of groceries you're hoisting out of your Connecticut-perfect wood-paneled station wagon. You're much better off with outfits that show off your body lines a little better (or, if your diet keeps starting "tomorrow," with clothes that give you a long, lean line).

Once you've gotten a basic sense of what your "look" is, heighten it with your accessories. For men, again, this means ties; women have more options. (If you're a man reading this, who thinks life's unfair, I'll invite you to trade places, for just a minute, with any woman who's ever had to wait a week to see if you're going to call her again after that first date. Even without costume jewelry and scarves to choose from, you guys are getting off easy.)

Accessories are the one category in which impulse buying isn't foolish. When you see a silk scarf or a necktie that makes your eyes sing and incorporates the exact shade of royal blue as the flecks in your tweed slacks, snap it up. Do not pass Go. (But do not spend $200; that's not Monopoly money you're handing over to the salesperson!)

As important as it is to dress like a "real person," and to fit in with your industry, don't fall prey to affectations. A few years ago, every male on "the Street" (yes, lingo can be affected, as well!) started wearing suspenders. A guy I knew, who was working for one of the big investment houses, started wearing them, too—until a senior partner pulled him aside and told him he hadn't been at the firm long enough to dress like a big shot. It was a joke . . . but it wasn't. Don't try to look like the stereotype of your industry's hotshots. Try to look like yourself. Your best self. Because when you look good, you feel good, and when you feel good about yourself, others can't help feeling good about you, too.

3

Playing It the Company Way

Understanding and Fitting In with Your Company's Culture

"Corporate culture" has nothing at all to do with whether they serve yogurt in the cafeteria. But the lunchroom *is* a good place to check it out. Corporate culture doesn't refer to the art magazines on the waiting-room table. But these, too, are good clues. What corporate culture *is*, according to cultural anthropologist Steve Barnett, Ph.D., is "the rules, values, and symbols that underlie and determine how corporate decisions are made and how everyday life in a company is experienced."

One good way to take your company's pulse is to read its printed materials. Annual reports, if issued, should give you a pretty clear idea of how the company wants outsiders to perceive it. Perhaps more important, though, are the newsletters and bulletins that land in your in-box. According to Judith C. Spear, Communications Manager for Westwood

Pharmaceuticals in Buffalo, New York, your company's magazines and newsletters can help you figure out what the organization expects of its employees, and how you should behave if you want to drive in the firm's fast track.

"Anything that's in your company newsletter is there because senior management wants it there," says Spear. "You can learn a lot both from what is in the newsletter and from what is omitted. You should be able to get an idea of who the company's heroes are," she says. Is the emphasis only on directors and managers, or is attention paid to lower-level employees as well? Does the company reward innovative thinking and problem solving? How much attention do they give people who have won industry awards or recognition? Or are kudos given only to those whose work shows an immediate impact on profits?

Most companies claim to value creativity. But if the "employee of the month" column is regularly devoted to those who have played it safe and toed the corporate line, the truth may differ from the advertising.

If the "heroes" are executives who come early, stay late, and never interrupt their work even to hit the washroom, yours is a real nose-to-the-grindstone office, and you're wise to behave accordingly. If the celebrities are recognized for their work in charity organizations, industry committees, and office events, you're working at a place that recognizes that staff members' outside interests can enhance the value of the work they perform between 9:00 and 5:00. What kind of activities are *you* involved in, and who knows about them?

Judi Spear says that the same publications that help you learn about the company you work for are an excellent way to let the company you work for learn about *you*. She advises you to wait about three months before trying to get into the company newsletter; it will take you that long to get a true sense of what sort of stories they're looking for. If you do have a story that you think is worth printing, check with your supervisor before approaching the newsletter editor. No one likes to feel he's being circumvented. If the editor is interested in your story, but doesn't have the time to devote to it, offer to write the piece yourself. Your best bet yet, says Spear, is to write a by-lined column on an area that affects the company. Of course, if you're the writer, you can't be the star (tacky, tacky!). But it doesn't matter—having a column is the ideal way to have your name known and associated with positive stories, regardless of whether they are about you. Just be sure to stay away from what corporate communicators call "Joe's fish" stories. No one cares how big that striped bass you caught was, or that your church bowling team made it to the semifinals. The stories you're pitching should relate in some way to values the company rewards, and should present you in only the most positive, professional light.

In addition to keeping your eyes and hands on the corporate newsletter, there are many other ways to read and enmesh yourself in your corporation's culture:

For example, take a good look at office manners and protocol. Does everyone call the boss Alvin, or is he Mr. Chipmunk? A firm where everyone is addressed by his courtesy title is probably more laced-up than an office in which workers refer to each other as "Hey, you." It's also more likely that the senior management is willing to listen to younger employees if they haven't set up an official barrier between the "misters" and the "regular Joes."

How important is promptness? I was raised by a woman who wears a watch in the bathtub. As a result, I've only been late once in my life—when the conductor of a train I was riding had a heart attack between New Haven and Hartford. (Despite the hour's train delay, I arrived at my destination only fifteen minutes late; I had left time for traffic.) I would have thought this quality would be lauded in the workplace, but noooo. . . . At the PR firm where I spent my first years after school, management assumed that if you could show up for a 10:00 meeting before 10:30, you weren't busy enough. It took me a while, but I finally figured out that the first one in the conference room was a rotten egg.

At other companies, tardiness is viewed as a lack of responsibility or concern for the schedules of others. Try to figure out how things work where *you* work, and learn to play the game.

Learn, too, how many innings you're expected to play for. Is staying late taken as a sign of dedication, or inefficiency? If staying late earns you Brownie points, do so at least a couple of nights a week. If you're such an efficient worker that by 5:30 there's nothing left for you possibly to do, hang around and look busy reading industry journals. Be sure to look engrossed when Mr. Chipmunk walks by. This will serve the dual purpose of keeping you abreast of what's new in the field and ensuring you're employed long enough to see the innovations you're reading about actually implemented.

Are your company's stars frantic fellows, or calm as Buddha himself? Are you expected to keep your cool and stifle your complaints, or is it *de rigueur* to hang out by the water cooler and compare war stories: "I was here till 1:00 A.M. . . ." "Oh, yeah, well, I had to work all weekend." "I'm sooo swamped!"

Again, learn to play the game. If everyone else acts graceful under pressure, so must you. If panic and fatigue are seen as a sign of creative genius, feign it if you must.

You must answer these questions about your company's personality repeatedly throughout your career. The answers might change when you get promoted, or when your boss does. A new boss is a sure harbinger of change, and a buy-out or merger can render all previous answers obsolete.

Lynn Black worked at a magazine for a year, and enjoyed the publisher's laid-back attitude. The staff was diligent, yet informal. The dress code was loose. Hours were flexible. Then, the magazine moved to the corporate headquarters of the conglomerate that owns it. While the publication looks the same to anyone who picks it up on the newsstand, the view from inside is quite different. Lynn's casual pants now hang at the back of her closet, while the front hangers are filled with corporate dresses and skirts. Instead of having only three bosses, she has thirty—many of whom she's never met. While Lynn still likes her job, she's aware of the fact that she's entered a whole new playing field. By going with the flow, rather than fighting the changes, she's managed to keep winning, and to talk new management into a hefty promotion and a raise to match.

The changes in office style can be equally dramatic if you're changing departments or office branches. When I switched groups at my PR agency, I naïvely assumed I'd just be praying in a different pew of the same church. In truth, the interdepartmental switch was more like indoctrination into a new religion. There were new commandments to follow, new gods to worship, and new catechisms to recite. After two months of trying to adjust, what I prayed for most was vacation. Getting the hang of my new department was tougher than acclimating to the company when I began my first position and had no preconceived (and wrong) notions tripping me up!!

Another example: Barry Rose was transferred from the Chicago branch of an ad agency to its New York affiliate. He figured the offices would be as similar as their competitive, urban surroundings. He figured wrong. In the midwest office, the only one around after 5:00 is the night watchman. At the Madison Avenue outpost, the copywriters are just swinging into creative gear at the cocktail hour. Barry says neither office is better or worse—they're just different.

Whether you're trying to decipher your company's code and make it spell "success!" for the first time or the twenty-first, executive-manners expert Letitia Baldrige offers the following additional suggestions for playing and winning the office game:

- When you start a new job, listen and learn; don't start talking before you have something worthwhile to say.
- Be nice to everyone; don't make snap judgments about whom you like, or about whom you want to like *you*. You never know whom you'll end up socializing with, working with, or working for—or depending on. Therefore, if you have a secretary, be sure to get on her good side immediately. Without her good graces, you'll get half as much done in twice the amount of time.

4

Do As I Say . . . *and* As I Do

Finding and Learning From a Mentor

Your "friends" aren't only those with whom you share confidences and beer. Often, the best "friend" you have at the office is someone with whom you don't share your personal life at all: a boss or colleague who has, for one altruistic reason or another, decided to take you under her wing and show you the ropes. In fact, one of the best ways to learn the corporate ropes and to climb swiftly is to learn from a pro—someone who has already succeeded in your field and your organization. A friend, a teacher, a mentor.

After you've been on the job awhile, you'll realize that the office environment sparks more unanswered questions in your mind than that grad-level philosophy course you took senior year. The work world can be confusing and confounding. And, confound it, there are no free departmental tutors. Or are there? Is there someone above you who seems to be taking an interest in your work and in seeing you succeed? Is there someone whose style you admire and wish to emulate? Is there someone who recognizes that the best way to lead is to teach, and that the best people to teach are those who are young, bright, and eager—like you? This person may make an ideal mentor, and can greatly enhance your ability to absorb new skills and workplace savvy.

According to experts at Catalyst, the national not-for-profit organization that works with corporations and individuals to develop career and family options, good mentoring serves not only the protégé, but the mentor and the organization as a whole. As a result, several companies are instituting formalized mentor programs, and many law firms assign "big siblings" to first-year associates.

What if your company has no such program? You can't just knock on doors and ask for willing volunteers. But you can make yourself visible to a superior by dint of your hard work and pleasant personality, thus inspiring her to take you under her wing. If you have true star potential, a wise boss will grab the opportunity to teach you and mold you. In addition to the satisfaction he'll derive, when you're on the cover of *Forbes*, in commenting that he "knew you when," mentorship will also almost guarantee your boss a topflight worker. Your talent and youthful enthusiasm, combined with his knowledge of the field, will help to make you the team member the other captains want to pick first; only he'll already have you fielding for *his* team.

The development of a mutually beneficial mentor relationship rests on your willingness to work hard, to observe, and to learn . . . and to take your mentor's constructive criticism in the spirit it's meant. According to criticism and stress expert Dr. Deborah Bright, you must remember that as a receiver of criticism, you are still in control. Do you accept the criticism? Can you learn from it? Will accommodating yourself to the criticizer's suggestions bring you closer to a goal? If the criticism you've been given is vague, ask for more specifics. Make the giver feel comfortable; don't become defensive. Your receptivity will encourage your mentor to continue giving you both negative and positive feedback.

If someone at the company has taken you on as a "project," you do owe a sense of loyalty and cooperation. Someone who is investing time and energy in teaching you everything you need to know deserves your best work, and a commitment to making her investment pay off. You demonstrate this by asking questions and putting the answers to work, and by being diligent.

You do *not* have to (nor should you) demonstrate your gratitude by sleeping with your boss or by pursuing any other course of action that could be detrimental to your career or self-esteem. Just because the head of cost accounting has invested five years teaching you everything he knows about process costing doesn't mean that you should pass up the opportunity to switch jobs and double your salary at another firm. If you've been playing the mentor game correctly, you've been paying your boss back for his or her support with your good work all along. You don't need to martyr yourself or your aspirations on an altar of misplaced gratitude. A good mentor will take pride in your achievements, wherever you achieve them. You may never be able to pay your first boss back for everything he taught you, but you can put in what you've gotten out by resolving to be that helpful to and supportive of those *you* ultimately supervise. Maintaining a chain of excellence in this way can be your biggest contribution to the long-term success of your company, and can also give you the psychic rewards of knowing you've helped nurture next year's young sapling.

Whether your first brush with direction giving is directed at a new hire or at your secretary, assistant, or co-worker, it should be done as politely but firmly as possible. The first intern I had to supervise, after a year at my first job, was someone I had known in college. So, to compound the fact that I had never been anyone's boss before, I was faced with the unpleasant task of delegating my unpleasant tasks to a friend. Barking orders is not my style, no matter whom I'm addressing. But, in this case, I leaned over just a bit too far in the other direction.

"I hate to ask you this," I'd start, "but would you mind terribly if I asked you to write a letter to the client and ask him to furnish us with the latest sales figures? You'll do it? Oh!! Thank you!!" After a few weeks, I realized that if she *did* mind, she had no business being in our business. Clearly, the problem was my own.

After struggling to effect the proper demeanor with my intern (and our secretary), I hit upon a technique I shared with the former, when she was having trouble with the latter. My big trick? Pretend you're asking your underling to pass the butter. Sounds crazy, I know. But it works—and so will the people you try it on.

When you ask someone to pass the butter at dinner, you and he both know that he should comply. Indeed, there is no doubt he will. You are asking someone to do that which society dictates they must, and for good reason. Still, you ask politely and quietly, because you are a polite and quiet person. (I, on the other hand, ask politely and loudly. I am not a quiet person.)

Similarly, when you ask your secretary to type a mailing

list, you both know he should. You both know he will. You are asking him to do that which his job dictates, and for good reason. Still, you ask politely and quietly, because . . . well, you know why.

After sharing this trick with my friend/intern, she told me that I was her role model. Now *that* is gratifying.

5

Meet Me in the Conference Room

Managing the Office Romance

Once you've learned how to fit in on the company playing field, you can decide whether it's best to play singles . . . or doubles. Depending on the kind of place you work in and the way you handle your fling, starting an office romance can be either the best reason to come to work on Monday mornings or the fastest way to ruin your career.

"Having an office romance is a great idea," says Eileen Marshall, "*if* you're planning on leaving the office." Marshall broke off her relationship with one of her co-workers in a sales-training program because "everyone knew our business. It made it really hard to act professional when everyone was asking at the Monday-morning meetings 'So, what did you two do this weekend?' " When Eileen quit her sales job for a position with another company, her relationship resumed—and deepened. "It was great that we met at work," she says. "It's even greater that I don't have to spend my office hours having lovers' quarrels anymore."

If you do tend to be quarrelsome in love, you'd best keep your passion out of the office. Patsi Shamus recalls with horror that "dating Anton [a co-worker] was a disaster. We would fight, scream, and slam doors. When I think back on it, I'm mortified." And the plot thickens. While Patsi and Anton were throwing crockery, a new group of trainees entered the ranks at their office. One of the new recruits was assigned to split her time between two departments. Her two bosses? You guessed it: Patsi and Anton. In what is probably the stupidest move on record, Carrie (the new recruit) made a play for Anton. Though he technically had a nonexclusive setup with Patsi, Anton was the worst choice Carrie could make. Talk about a lose-lose situation: if things worked out with Anton, she was sure to be Patsi's least favorite trainee. If the romance fizzled, Anton wouldn't be singing her praises too highly. What happened? you ask. Only the worst. Carrie's fling with Anton lasted just long enough to anger Patsi, and soured in time to turn Anton against Carrie as well. Are you surprised to hear that within four months, Carrie had changed jobs? She hadn't been fired . . . but she wasn't made to feel too welcome, either.

But wait. Before you give up, hear some (condensed) happy-ever-after tales of love at the water cooler. One of my clients married her boss. My friend's brother and sister-in-law met when they summer-clerked for the same judge during law school. Two executives in my old company have recently wed, with blessings—and a very nice present—from the chairman.

If you are tempted to pursue an office romance, Letitia Baldrige cautions you to keep it *out* of the office. "It's great to be attracted to someone,'' she says. ''Just make sure you don't show it during working hours. Your company is not paying you to spend their valuable time exercising your libido.''

Far simpler than office romances (thank goodness!) are office friendships. In chapter 14 of this book, I explain in greater detail how making friends with your co-workers can enhance your personal life.

6

How to Succeed in Business? Really Trying!

Keeping Your Shoulder to the Wheel

All of the foregoing tips and tricks will help you fit in at the office and will help smooth your path to success. Success, though, takes far more than wearing the right tie or hitching your wagon to the right star. To get good results, you have to be *good.* You have to work hard, and you have to be willing to learn.

Calvin Coolidge said, "Nothing takes the place of persistence." And along with persistence, you need perseverance, elbow grease, and stick-to-it-iveness. Get the picture?

Beyond the hard work you put in at the office, you can speed your ascent by keeping up-to-date on all innovations in your field, and by reading as many professional journals as you can get your hands on. Also be sure to keep yourself well informed about current events, and to know how these will affect your industry, your company, and its customers.

Eleanor Raynolds, C.B.E., co-author of *Beyond Success: How Volunteer Service Can Help You Begin Making a Life Instead of Just a Living* (MasterMedia), says that working for a nonprofit organization after hours can give your career a boost as well. "When you look at any real leader," she says, "you will discover that they are involved in volunteer organizations. A true leader gives back." All the better if you can give back with your professional expertise. If you're a teacher, try a tutoring program for underprivileged kids. If you work in advertising or PR, lend your creative talents to an organization that can use some publicity. Help a company keep its financial records to maintain not-for-profit status. Use whatever you do well to help you do good.

Another way to up your visibility is to join the appropriate professional associations. Even if you don't go to every meeting, you should try to get to know as many colleagues as you can. You can share on-the-job tips with one another, and learn about opportunities at other companies. If you are dedicated to staying at your own company, interfacing with colleagues at others can help you learn what the competition is up to.

According to experts at the National Association of Female Executives (NAFE), you should try to develop as many different networks as possible, to include executives who do exactly what you do; those in other fields that touch on yours, or that you think you might be interested in down the road; workers your own age and at your general level of professional accomplishment; and those who have been out in the work world for a while and will be able to share their experiences with you. (For more on this last group, see chapter 4, on finding a mentor.)

These networks may be informal, but often they will grow out of your participation in industry groups or groups, like NAFE, that are established expressly for the purpose of fostering strong networks. When joining a networking or professional support group, you should expect both contacts and information. In exchange for this, you have to respect the networking process, and those you're asking for information. There's nothing wrong with making it clear that your interest in someone lies in how they can help your career, as long as you accept the fact that turnabout is fair play. (What can you do for them? What will you be willing to do for a younger worker five or ten years down the line?)

When you're pursuing a business contact for advice or information, NAFE advises you to remember the following:

Have respect for the businessperson's time; don't take up too much of it, or contact someone at a time that's not convenient (remember your time zones, unless you want to be hung up on by a ranting roommate when you've forgotten that it's after midnight out East or before dawn on the West Coast).

If you're a woman, it's especially important to find a women's network group (either a general one, like NAFE, or an industry-specific one, like Advertising Women of New York—or both). As far as the cigarette ads say we've come, baby, there's still a long way to go, and an old boy network that's tighter than your jeans from junior high school.

Your local library will have copies of an association directory; do some research, and ask around in your office: What groups do people belong to? How do you join? The membership fees you invest will pay off many times over in the contacts you make and information you pick up. (And speaking of picking up, it's not unlikely that that cute person you spy across the reception room at your association meeting has at least some of the same interests as you. . . .)

If your company offers training and development sessions, go—even if they are optional. You'll probably learn something, and you'll certainly peg yourself as someone who's interested in doing well.

Ron Carzoli, a human resources expert, says that the difference between a good worker who advances quickly and one who doesn't is the ability to sell ideas. "You have to have confidence in your ideas, and the ability to sell them," he says, noting that it's only natural to be hesitant at first. "A true leader," he says, "is smart enough to look at a problem creatively in the first place, and then wise enough to know how to articulate or write those ideas down, and, finally, to sell them."

One good opportunity to sell your ideas is at staff meetings. "If you are a participant," write Beverly Benz Treuille and Susan Schiffer Stautberg in *Managing It All* (MasterMedia), "do your homework. It's your chance to shine before your colleagues and superiors. If you have a valid point to make, raise it as soon as you can. Try to present it as an outgrowth of the discussion to which the team contributed, not your own proprietary idea. If you feel you must express disagreement, be conscious of the other person's need to save face and do it with tact."

When jobs and money are tight, it's more important than ever to keep yourself flexible and marketable. In other words, in addition to working harder, you've got to work *smarter*. In the October 1991 issue of *Business Week*, writer Bruce Nussbaum recommends taking the following steps to help keep yourself employable and promotable:

- Build skills. Forget about titles; skills are what give you the mobility to change divisions, companies, or even industries.

- Moonlight. It's a way to develop those precious skills.
- Learn. Get an MBA or take enrichment programs. The more you know, the more jobs will be open to you.

Keep learning, keep trying, and keep the above in mind and you're sure to do well.

7

Sir, Could I Please Have . . . More?

Asking For and Getting Your First Raise

In economic boom times, the reward for a job well done was a raise. In a recession, more often, the reward for a job well done is . . . a job. With hiring freezes and layoffs the rule rather than the exception, raises are becoming rarer—and smaller—than hen's teeth. According to the U.S. Bureau of Labor statistics, annual merit raises are not even keeping pace with the cost of living index. Many companies have even implemented across-the-board salary cuts. But this doesn't make you, the hardworking employee, one bit less anxious for a raise, now, does it?

Of course not. Like everyone else in this (increasingly capitalistic) world, you surely want to be compensated for all your hard work. Good news: Even in the toughest of times, it is possible to get more money (or, at least, better perks) if you have proven yourself valuable to your company . . . and if you sharpen your negotiating skills.

Most companies will tell you when you're hired how soon you'll be up for review, and unless you hear otherwise in the interim, the review process will proceed on schedule. Usually, new employees are up for review after six months. If your company *does* have a set review schedule, you're ahead of the game. In a sense, the door has been opened for you: when your six-month anniversary comes around and you get a glowing (we hope) review, you can segue neatly into a raise negotiation.

Small companies are less likely than large conglomerates to have etched-in-stone review and raise schedules, but this can often work to your advantage. Unlike the mammoth manufacturer that can't give you a raise without giving pay increases to your twenty-five equally talented counterparts, a small company *can* give just you a raise if just you have a particular title or area of responsibility.

According to Tessa Albert Warschaw, Ph.D., author of *Winning by Negotiation* (McGraw-Hill), timing is the single most important influence on your chances of getting that raise or those perks. Before sauntering into your boss's office and asking for a pay hike, consider how your request jibes with current events on the office front. Are mass layoffs under way? Better wait until the dust has settled. Did the company just post record profits? Time is on your side, especially if your department has been credited with the company's success.

Also consider your boss's personal mood. Has she just lost an important pitch for new business? She probably won't be too anxious to sit down and talk about how she can improve your standard of living. Was he just elected employee of the year? Charge ahead; he's probably feeling more benevolent than usual.

A note of caution: There are some conditions under which the appearance of ideal timing can be deceptive. If you've just been handed an extra project because the firm is bringing in business faster than anyone anticipated, you're wise to ask for a raise. However, if your newly increased workload is the result of someone else's non-work-related misfortune (broken hip, nervous breakdown), it's best to hang out awhile before asking for the extra cash. Otherwise, you're likely to look like an opportunist, not a team player. *After* several weeks or months of proving you can handle the added responsibility, you can ask to be duly compensated.

Once the timing's right, you can work on polishing your request so that it is concise and convincing. What have you done, and how well? Have clients or customers written you letters of praise, or complimented you verbally on the professionalism with which you handled their projects? Have your good ideas made the department more productive or profitable? Be prepared to blow your own horn; this is no time for modesty.

But before you waste your "why I deserve a raise" speech on the wrong person, be sure you know the proper protocol at your firm. Does your direct supervisor decide on your salary? Does he or she negotiate for you (or against you, as the case may be) with upper management? Or do you have to meet with the big guns yourself, and convince people who've never seen you in action that your piece of the action should be bigger?

Once you know whom you'll be talking to, try to anticipate what kind of negotiator he or she is. If he/she is what Dr. Warschaw calls a Big Mama/Big Daddy negotiator—one who likes to manipulate like the worst kind of parent—you're wise to pepper your spiel with references to everything you've learned at the feet of this pinstriped guru.

Insert references to how your work together has allowed you to gather the experience and skill that warrant your raise. Schmaltz it up.

If you're dealing with what Dr. Warschaw calls a "jungle fighter," be prepared for a showdown that would frighten Tarzan himself. Don't get argumentative or hostile. Just get tough. The more hard facts—industry standards, office policies, departmental precedents—you arm yourself with, the better you'll be able to counter your boss's objections.

In short, you need to understand your boss's psyche to psych him into giving you the raise you so richly deserve.

Ready, now? Good. Next stop: your boss's office.

"Now that I've been here six months," you might say, "I'd like a chance to discuss with you how things are going, and to talk about the areas in which I can begin to assume more responsibility."

This "I've been here six months" strategy will highlight your impressive ability to read a calendar. (That's cause for a merit increase, right there!) It will also demonstrate your initiative and eagerness. So far, you're batting a thousand. Ask the boss when a good time to discuss this would be. Be prepared to list a few areas where you'd like more responsibilities. Which tasks would you like to begin delegating to a newer-comer so that you can turn your attention to more complicated issues, and remove some of the burden from your boss's shoulders?

You should also be armed with knowledge of what you can fairly expect to be earning. What do people in your position at other companies pull down? Do you know what your interdepartmental counterparts are paid at your own company? Has your company given other raises this year? Having a general sense of what the market will bear guarantees that you will neither undersell yourself nor lose your credibility by asking for three times what you're worth.

Whether your performance review is self-initiated or part of the organizational structure, it'll come as no surprise to your boss when you bring up money. While this may be the first time *you're* asking for a raise, rest assured it's not your boss's maiden voyage down negotiation lane. Be confident and firm. Do *not*, under any circumstances, apologize when asking for a raise. Even in a recession, you're entitled to be paid fairly, but no one is going to hand you your raise on a silver platter. Once you've done your homework about what you can honestly expect to make, ask for a couple of thousand dollars more than that. This will allow your boss to save face by "making you compromise." Everyone does this, and everyone knows everyone else does it, but no one wants to be the first to stop.

Small companies and entrepreneurial ventures are also more likely to consider less-traditional methods of compensation. If the boss can't afford to give you a raise, maybe you can get extra paid-vacation time or a percentage of next year's profits—or maybe you can work out something *totally* off the wall, like having your globe-trotting boss give *you* some of her airline bonus miles for your personal use on vacation. (Even the largest companies are using these nontraditional compensation strategies to hold on to valued employees; according to an article in the September 1991 issue of *Working Woman* magazine, 29 percent of American companies reward their star performers by giving them either a block of company stock or a good purchase price if they wish to invest in it. Companies such as Borden, Inc., reward their employees with small treats—baseball tickets, dinners out—to let them know their above-the-call-of-duty efforts aren't going unnoticed.)

Sound convincing—and convince. If you sound unsure

about the merits of your request for more money, it's going to be a lot tougher to convince your boss. But be sure the "raisons de raise" you list are merit-related and need-blind. In other words, you're not asking for a raise because your rent was just hiked and the price of a beer has gone up to $4 at your favorite hangout. No. You're asking for more moola because you have (check one): (a) worked your ass off for it, (b) saved the company enough money by dint of your thrift and management skills that they were able to carpet the new Orlando office, or (c) done absolutely nothing of value but convinced everyone that the company can't function without you.

I got my first raise by employing a combination of tactics. First, I was in the right place at the right time. One of my supervisors had just announced that she wanted to leave corporate America for beachfront Greece, and would be leaving two of the accounts I worked on uncovered. Because these accounts were reasonably important to the department, and because I had just been offered a job by a competitive concern at a hefty pay increase, I was able to negotiate a serious promotion and a rather nice raise, several months before I was officially scheduled to receive either one. And just to prove that what goes around comes around, I was transferred to another department just when the woman who had bequeathed her spot to me had returned from Europe. She got her job back, at a much higher salary than she had left it, I got a challenging new assignment, and we all got a kick out of fate's strange sense of humor.

It's not always this easy, as I discovered when it came time to negotiate for my next raise. Different bosses, economic climates, and company politics can damn your chances of getting a raise you deserve. If cutbacks or company financial difficulties (or your boss's pigheadedness, for that matter) are making it impossible for him or her to come through with the bucks you rightfully deserve, do *not* become belligerent when you are offered the 59-cent booby prize.

When my PR training program was over, the program director called me to inform me that of the twelve trainees in my group, I was one of five invited to stay on at the firm. Due to some difficulties the agency had recently undergone, though, I would be raised not to the previously promised salary but to $5,000 less than that.

Though I was probably right to be outraged, I still regret shrieking, "My mother's *maid* makes more than that!"

I later understood this apparent discrepancy. The cleaning woman speaks no English. Therefore, she is unable to open the kind of wise-ass mouth to my mom that I did to my boss. No matter how insulted or angry you feel, keep your cool.

If the offer you've been made truly is insulting, you have two options: (1) quietly accept it or (2) quietly start looking elsewhere. Do *not* threaten to quit, unless you have another job lined up. Even if you do have something else available, do *not* storm out in a huff. Quietly explain that you've decided to pursue an opportunity elsewhere. Say that you'll be around for two more weeks, and could your boss please let you know how you can make things easiest for the next person who fills your job. You never know when you'll need a recommendation from these people. You never know when one of them will marry your sister's nephew and wind up on your right-hand side at every family wedding for the next thirty years. Be as professional walking out the door as you were coming in.

Fortunately, this leave-taking is almost never necessary.

If you're good at what you do, and have proven yourself a good "fit" with the company, they will want to keep you around. After all, they've just spent six months of their time and their money teaching you everything you (and, maybe, they) know. Chances are they don't want to see that investment walk out their door and through that of their biggest competitor.

8

Smooth Moves

Tricks to Make the Daily Grind Less Grinding

Remember when a "heavy load" meant taking a course with extra reading? Remember when "too much to handle" was a 9:00 class? Those are now, officially, the Good Old Days. All but one of my survey respondents said they find work more stressful than school—and that they find it very stressful indeed. The stress of work is compounded by the fear of *no* work, too. During mass layoffs, everyone feels the tension, even if you're still employed.

Dr. Deborah Bright, president of Bright Enterprises, an organization dedicated to quality education, says this stress can be minimized if you stop focusing on it. "If you're only looking at yourself, and at the short term," she says, "you're going to increase stress. Don't just focus on the stress you face today; see your current situation as a stepping stone toward something you want. Just as people go to the gym not for the immediate pain but for the long-term gain, remember when you get up to go to work that the unpleasant chore you face today is part of paying your dues to get where you want to go.

"Quit asking yourself how you *feel* about work," she continues, "and just do it!"

To make doing it easier, get yourself as organized as possible. And that means making the most of your time.

"Life is lived sequentially," write the authors of *Managing It All*. "Set time frames for your goals and periodically revise them. Break down a larger undertaking into manageable segments. Divide a major assignment that is on your projects list into day-by-day tasks. Set your deadline, and then work backward from that date. Plan to do a little each day in a logical sequence until the project is completed. Build in time for unavoidable delays."

If you want to make the most of your time, take a good look at how you waste it. Do you spend fifteen minutes a day walking to the water fountain and back? Get an attractive, insulated jug and fill it up each morning. Do you spend hours trying to find mislabeled files? Take one Sunday morning in the office with no one around to redo your system, thus saving yourself many times over the number of hours you've invested.

Think of your lunch hour as the perfect time to get things done. Use it for personal or work-related activities, or maybe a trip to the gym. Similarly, your commuting time can be put to good use: walk to work and get some exercise, or write letters to old friends while you sit on the bus. If you drive to work, listen to books on tape.

Finally, take some valuable time out to decompress, and be sure to give yourself a break when you really need it. Dr. Bright says you should admit the stress is too much for you to handle when you develop physical symptoms, or when what should be normal wear and tear is tearing you apart.

You can reduce stress by learning what causes it. Not everyone is affected in the same way by similar events. Try to figure out what bothers you and, if you can, avoid it. If you can't avoid it, try laughing at it. A healthy dose of humor makes even the toughest situation a little easier on the nerves.

9

Can This Marriage Be Saved?

What to Do If You Hate Your Job . . . or Your Boss

Three years ago, I advised employees who hated their jobs to leave them. If I did that today, I'd end up the first author ever to be sued for malpractice.

Unless your job is absolutely unbearable, you're well advised to wait it out until the job market opens up, for several reasons: first of all, a company that's firing is most likely to give the axe to an employee they suspect is looking elsewhere. Rob Mulroney, who has worked in corporate banking for five years, was about to start looking for a job in personal banking until his bank started laying off employees. "Look," he told me, "they've fired fifteen people so far, a lot of whom were doing decent work. If they know I'm looking to leave, they'll fire me next. 'After all,' they'll say, 'why fire someone else who wants to stay here, if Rob's going to be gone in a few months anyway? Let's get rid of him, and let the other guy keep his job.' " There are few secrets in corporate America, and *someone* at your company is sure to find out you're job hunting. Unless you're willing to risk parting company on *their* schedule rather than *yours,* don't jeopardize your secure job just because you think you might be happier with a shorter commute or a better company cafeteria. (On the flip side, if your job is in *real* jeopardy, it's wise to have your ducks in a row for a possible job hunt. Don't start sending out résumés, but do make a list of people you might contact if you lose your job, and spend as much time as you can networking. Even if you never do get laid off, it never hurts to know more people.)

Even if you *can* find another job without your superiors knowing it, you had better be sure the company you're moving *to* can keep you employed. Last year, my friend Alan decided that he'd had enough of the law firm he'd been working at, and he started looking for a job in marketing, in which he'd gotten his undergraduate degree. It took almost a year, but finally, he landed a position with a small consulting firm. He'd be cutting his salary in half, but he was excited. Though the law firm begged him to stay and even offered him a raise (a rarity in this economy!), Alan stuck to his guns and accepted the position. He cleared out his desk, went on vacation, and came back ready to start his new job. Only there was a hitch: when he returned, he found on his answering machine a message from the marketing firm, saying that they'd just lost their biggest client and, therefore, would be unable to give Alan the job they'd promised him. Since he had already been hired, this counted as being fired, and Alan was able to collect unemployment for six months. Needless to say, he had a hard time making ends meet and an even harder time finding a new job. The entry-level marketing spot he finally landed paid less than both his law job and the marketing job for which he had left the firm, and it took him quite a while to recover from the stress of being unemployed for so long.

I relate these horror stories not to ruin your day but to drive home a point. Gone are the days when a rival job offer was the best way to get a raise. Today, it's the cleanest, least painful way for your original company to get one employee off the payroll. So be sure to think long and hard before you start job hunting. Instead, work to make your solution more livable:

Identify what's really bothering you. Is it the work itself? See if you can take on some responsibilities in another area of your company. This may mean more work overall, but an interesting ten-hour workday beats a boring nine-to-fiver every time.

Do you just need a change of scenery? Keep your ears open for international assignments. I know a woman who spent six months in South Africa and one who just left for a half-year in Budapest, each working on a short-term project for her own firm. With all the changes in Europe, many companies are opening offices there. Let the appropriate decision-makers know you'd be willing to work abroad for a while. Surprisingly, it's not always easy to find volunteers. (Married workers and those with other family responsibilities are often reluctant to pull up their stakes.)

If your boss is your problem, you may have a tougher time, but there are things you can do to improve office relations. Lawrence J. Bradford and Claire Raines, the authors of *Twentysomething: America's New Work Force* (MasterMedia), offer the following tips for bridging the "attitude gap" between the career-obsessed yuppies many of us work for and our own feelings that our jobs owe *us* something, too:

- Understand value differences: know what your own values are . . . and find out about your boss's. Remember that supervisors are often tremendously loyal to the company. They may not admit it, but for many of them, their jobs are the most important things in their lives. If that's not true for you, you don't have to change, but respect the difference and tread lightly on the loyalty issue.
- Be patient. It takes time to prove you're good and to begin achieving career success. Most bosses will expect you to "pay your dues" before giving you the projects you want and the recognition you deserve.
- Express yourself. Let your boss and co-workers get to know you. Tell them and show them what's important to you.

But when you want to express yourself, don't just blurt out your opinions. Plan your presentation to your boss as you would a pitch to a client. Coolheaded communications are *especially* important if your office-place "opinion gap" has already progressed to the "problem" stage.

If you've been having trouble communicating with your boss, employee communications specialist Amy Juskowitz suggests you set up an appointment to talk to him about how you can improve your communications. ("Don't go in unannounced and bring the topic up," she warns. "It will put your boss on the defensive.") Set clear goals and objectives for ways you can make projects run more smoothly—does your boss want you to keep her more up-to-date? Handle your projects more autonomously? Often, "boss problems" stem from simple misunderstandings about what it is your boss expects from you.

Even if this doesn't work, Juskowitz advises, don't go

around badmouthing your boss. "It will come back in your face over and over again," she cautions. While you're holding your tongue, keep yourself busy outside of the office. When you have a job you can't stand, it's more important than ever to get satisfaction outside of the office. Develop a good support system and get involved in a project that will provide you with the positive reinforcement your boss won't dish out. Whether it's volunteering in a local soup kitchen or tackling a home-repair project you've been putting off, doing something you can be proud of *outside* work will help make you a little less miserable during office hours, too.

If all this fails, or if you're so miserable that one more day at your job seems like a death sentence, forget all the foregoing advice and job hunt, recession or no recession. Worse comes to worst, you too can tend lobsters in a pound.

10

So the Month Doesn't Last Longer Than the Money

Developing and Sticking to a Budget

I was not written up in *Working Woman* magazine because of the inestimable contributions I had made to the science of water-cooler etiquette. Nor was it my staple-removing acumen they featured, maybe in a piece called "Office Supply Management."

"Early last summer," my write-up began, "Susan Kleinman, an account executive with Ruder Finn & Rotman, Inc., a public relations firm in New York, found herself discussing salaries over drinks in a trendy café. Her date, an investment banker, makes double her salary. 'I told him how hard it is for me to save money,' says Kleinman. 'And he said he doesn't save anything, either.' "

To disprove the article's reputation-damaging insinuation that I am unable to save anything, I have preserved the December issue that carries my name. I think it's a start.

Psychologists and economists have identified several explanations for the inability to save money. "Fear of success!" the pop shrinks affirm; "The declining value of the dollar," say the money mavens. The true explanation is really far simpler than that. I make too little and spend too much.

"What you need is a budget," said my father, the CPA, denying my third request in three months for "just a little loan until my next paycheck."

What I need, I countered, silently, is a father who will dole out endless supplies of cash, and ask for nothing in return but a postcard from the Caribbean isle where I'm vacationing on his credit card.

Failing a trust fund ("You *have* a trust fund," my dad says. "I *trust* you to make your own funds"), you are going to have to establish a budget for yourself.

Needless to say, my father had a few suggestions.

"In planning a budget," he said, "you have to remember that the number of places you find to spend money rises at least as fast as the availability of the funds."

This would explain why the date of *Working Woman* fame saves no more money than I do, despite the difference in our salaries. In fact, if I understand Dad correctly (and he made sure that I would), the more money you make, the more likely it is you'll end up overspending.

Need proof? If you take $100 out of the bank on Monday, and plan on its lasting you till Friday, you should have $60 left Wednesday morning. I'll bet you next week's allowance, though, that by Wednesday, you're at least two-thirds through the money. Yet, somehow, you still have *some* left on Friday. As your wallet shrinks or expands, so do your expenditures.

There are two ways to keep your expenses better regulated, says Dad (Bernie, to you). The first way, unfortunately, doesn't work.

"Forget about writing down in a notebook every newspaper and stick of gum you buy and trying to develop spending limits from that," he says. "That system last three days —and then only if you're incredibly compulsive."

Many banks with personal finance departments have special booklets in which you can keep track of the purchase price of your Kleenex. These will make you no more diligent —just more remorseful every time you notice the unused dinero-diary lying fallow on your kitchen counter.

"Instead, to avoid spending your money, make your disposable funds less accessible," says Bernie. "To save for a major purchase (car, vacation, apartment, stereo) or investment, develop a self-taxing system. Every time you get a paycheck, immediately withdraw a percentage of your net pay—this shouldn't be less than 5 percent and should optimally be 10 percent. Deposit this money into a separate, interest-bearing account like a money market or a regular savings account."

Unfortunately, I didn't ask Bernie for his advice until I was drafting this chapter. After six months on the job, I realized that I had not yet stuffed a single dime into my mattress, and decided to check out my savings options. I figured that if I stuck to my budget (a little tougher than sticking to a greasy pole on a hot day), I could save $100 a month. In three years, I could buy a new lamp.

I waltzed into my friendly neighborhood bank, and discovered that they are indeed a bank located in my neighborhood. But friendly? Forget it.

"Ya wanna start a savings account, ya need fivehunnert dollas," the teller told me (telled me?). If I had the talent and/or willpower to amass $500, would I need a savings account?

Contrary to logic, it turns out that most savings options —bank accounts, IRAs, money markets—require you to prove you don't really need them, anyway, by saving a little cash on your own, first. There is usually a minimum opening balance, and some also require that all subsequent deposits exceed a certain amount.

If necessary, stuff your weekly savings into a sock drawer before opening an account. A saner, but more easily way-laid, system is to let the opening balance accrue (untouched!) in your checking account. Transfer it to savings as soon as you have the minimum. The problem with this is that many unenforced savings plans, like every diet I've ever almost gone on, begin "tomorrow."

If you need motivation to let each week's contribution pile up in your account rather than finding its way into the hand of the record store owner or clothing salesman, consider this: if you start putting away $20 a week today, and leave it in an account that bears 5 percent interest compounded quarterly, you'll have a little more than $1,000 by the end of the year. By the end of five years, your balance should be about $5,866.

The opening balances for money market funds tend to be higher. But, then, the interest is usually greater as well. Hard as it may be to accrue an opening balance, financial planner Judith Briles strongly recommends opening a money market fund. "Having a money market fund means never having to say you're stuck," says Dr. Briles, author of *The Woman's Guide to Financial Savvy* and *The Dollars and Sense of Divorce.*

Briles also recommends you get an IRA even if you can't deduct it on your taxes. The laws keep changing, but as of this writing, IRAs were tax deferred. "It's important to make those commitments now," she says. "One problem among young adults is that it's tempting to fall into the *mañana* mentality—I'll start saving tomorrow—or the Scarlett O'Hara syndrome: tomorrow is another day."

The time to start saving is now—that proverbial rainy day may come sooner than you expected it. No matter how secure you feel in your job, and no matter how healthy you are, you could find yourself needing to draw on your savings after an unexpected setback knocks you flat.

When my friend Stacey, a nurse, jabbed herself with a hepatitis-positive needle on the job, she was out of work for eleven months. Fortunately (a relative term), the needle was infected with nothing more serious than hepatitis. Fortunately, too, her injury had occurred on the job, so she received a workmen's compensation package that actually exceeded her after-tax salary. The guy whose infected needle she got in the palm of her hand, though, *hadn't* gotten his disease on the job. Like him, you can get hepatitis, mono, or a dozen other ailments that will keep you out of work, and it's always best to be prepared.

According to Judith Briles, you should have enough money readily accessible to live on for three to six months. In calculating that figure, realize that this doesn't mean that many months' salary, but the amount you'll need to supplement unemployment or disability insurance (check with your employer on the extent to which you're covered) to equal your after-tax monthly net.

The most accessible place to stash your money without penalty for withdrawal at any time is a bank savings account. In general, these yield 5¼ percent, and your money is insured up to $100,000. Somehow, I don't think any of us have to worry about exceeding this insurable limit.

To make sure you're well covered in an emergency, keep one credit card (with a low annual fee, but a high credit limit) that you never use. There's nothing worse than trying to charge something in an emergency (e.g., plane fare home if there's a sudden need) only to discover that you're $53 away from your spending limit. This card should be backed with a reserve savings with which you can promptly pay off your emergency expenses.

While it's important to save for a "rainy day," you'll probably want to save a little for the sunshine, as well. Several banks have vacation savings plans. Like Christmas clubs, these accounts offer no extraordinary interest benefits. Many of them, though, withdraw an amount of your choice from your checking account each week. This is a formalized version of the self-taxing system described above. But instead of going to build aircraft carriers, or to buy $5,900 toilet seats for the Pentagon, this "withholding" goes toward getting *you* on a plane to somewhere warm where the rum punch flows as freely as government military funds. Your savings and investment options are more numerous and varied than the islands on which you can spend your hard-earned vacation.

To start making intelligent choices about where and how to divide and save your money, Dr. Briles recommends you start getting all the information you can, as soon as you can. She points out that many investment companies sponsor seminars to which they welcome new graduates. You should attend not with an eye to signing up for an investment right away, but as part of the education that will enable you to invest wisely.

You should also, says Dr. Briles, start learning immediately who the pros are. Get to understand what bankers, financial planners, insurance people, and brokers do even before you're ready to use them. When you're looking for financial advice, she says, "don't go to a rubber stamp person; there are plenty of experienced, talented people who specialize in handling smaller investors, and there are those who enjoy mentoring and seeing a young investor grow."

The sooner you understand your investment options, the more readily you can begin to plan for the future. My brother, Joey, who has tried unsuccessfully to teach me everything he learned at the Wharton School of Business, says that your best first investment, if you're less than confident, is a mutual fund. Someone who knows the ropes a little better than you chooses the buys and sells, and watches out for your interests. And your dividends.

If you're interested in mutual funds, check into their rankings by *Forbes* or *Fortune* magazine. Your broker (more about her in a minute) will be able to give you rankings and suggest funds as well.

If you are interested enough in investing to need a broker, you may want to check into the services offered by the discount brokerage houses (like Muriel Siebert & Co.). One of the benefits of the discount houses is that many allow you to call at all hours, so that you don't have to conduct your personal business from the office. The chairman of the board may look suave yelling orders through the phone to his broker; you'll look as if you're goofing off on company time.

If you'd like a little more hand-holding, and are willing to pay the higher commissions that are the price tag on this, contact a full-service broker. He or she can answer your questions, get you any research reports you might be interested in, and take some degree of responsibility for your account. A hidden benefit of having a personal relationship with a broker is that these guys know *everyone* and can be excellent contacts, very much worth cultivating.

Over time, the stock market performs better than any

other investment; even without splitting two-for-one, most stocks will be worth several times their purchase price by the time you retire. This has even been the case over decades when the market crashed; unless the crash happens the day before you retire, the stocks will come back—and then some—by the time you're ready to cash them in.

Don't feel, though, that you've *got* to get into the stock market, or into any other investment that you're not comfortable with or fully able to afford. "There's no law that everyone should be in the market," says Joey. "And it certainly isn't for blind gambling. If you're that hot on the idea of betting—and maybe losing—your shirt, go to Atlantic City. The stakes are smaller, and they sell hot dogs on the boardwalk."

Judith Briles agrees, and adds that even for those who are interested in investing in the stock market, there are times to stay out. "One thing to learn," she says, "is that times change very quickly; it's not always a good time to stay in the market. Any time you're uncertain is time to get out."

One friend of mine who dabbles in stocks sets a limit each time he invests: for each stock he purchases, he decides in advance what price he'll sell at. Say he buys the stock at 23⅛ and decides to sell when it hits 30; the day it hits 30, he sells, takes the money, and runs—at least far enough to call his girlfriend and tell her he's taking her out to dinner. He does *not* stay in in the hopes that the stock will rise to 103. Nor does he kick himself after he's sold and the stock is at 32. "I figure I made a 33 percent profit," he says. "When you get greedy is when you start to lose money and sleep."

11

There Must Be a Hole in My Wallet

Figuring Out Where Your Money Goes

Now that we've discussed some of the possibilities of what you can do with your self-levied tax rolls, we can return to budgeting that portion of your money that you actually get to *spend*.

"It's very simple, Sue," says my brother. "Just figure out how much you can afford to spend each week, and take that amount out of the bank on Monday. If you spend it before the week's up, tough shit."

John Maynard Keynes, eat your heart out.

Actually, Joey's advice is the most logical, and the best I've heard. It's amazing how much less "desperately" I need a fifth pair of black pumps on Tuesday when I know I'll have to cook them for dinner by Friday.

Judith Briles takes Joey's caveat one step further: while she advocates setting and sticking to a budget, she does *not* recommend that you use a cash card.

"They're an absolute disaster," she says of the magic plastic cards. "There's a $20 minimum withdrawal, and it's quicker to push the fast cash buttons for $40 or even $100. When you have extra money in your pocket," she cautions, "it goes straight to cash heaven."

In her financial planning practice, Briles would ask people where their money went. Those who had the least clear idea of the answer (my own best guess is that there are holes in my pockets) usually had cash cards.

Most weeks, even with my cash card, I do stick to my self-imposed allowance. To determine what yours should be, you'll have to sit down and figure out exactly how much you really earn, what your expenses are, and how you can economize. This process, like sit-ups, will probably hurt if you're doing it right.

It's very nice to read about how much you make in *Working Woman*. It would be nicer still to take more than half of that figure home. The most immutable portion of your budget, then, is Uncle Sam's cut. Unlike your relatives in the carpet and used-car businesses, this uncle doesn't make deals. Your after-tax paycheck is all you have to work with. Engrave that figure in your mind and at the top of the to-be-tearstained page on which you plan your monthly debits and credits.

Now, subtract your rent. (This sounds like a card trick, but it's not. If I knew tricks, I would make my money multiply like rabbits in a hat.) If the difference is a negative number, call home and hope that they haven't rented out your room quite yet.

An old rule of thumb was that your rent should equal one-quarter of your salary. (If you're reading this in Boston, you're laughing.) A newer guideline is that your rent should be no larger than the first of your two monthly paychecks, after taxes. (If you're reading *that* in Manhattan, you're crying.) Most realistically, your rent will equal that portion of your after-tax dollars that you can part with and not starve.

You have to pay for apartments and basic utilities on time, lest you lose them, so be sure they're the number-one item on your list.

If you have student loans to pay off, be mindful that the government is starting to crack down on loan leeches. And not only do you owe the bank. You also owe next year's crop of freshmen the same opportunities you had. End of sermon.

The encouraging thing about loan payments is that unlike grocery and doctor's bills, you *will* eventually be through paying them. This will probably happen just as your kid's nursery school tuition bills start pouring in, though. There is just no justice.

How much do you pay each month on your car? When computing this total, include not only loan payments but also parking costs, gas and oil expenses, and insurance premiums.

Expensive as city living is, and as bothersome as monthly payments can be, bearing those costs is not nearly as painful as the reality of where your money really goes. It's embarrassing to realize that a quarter of your take-home pay goes to taco chips.

You'll soon realize that you spend the most money on the things that give you the least pleasure. A woman with unbitten fingernails can count on snagging at least three pair of hose a week. Most men will pour money like Drano through the hungry pipes of the shirt launderer's emporium. Housecleaning supplies can eat up more than dust and grime, too. Somehow, though, a sparkling sink will not give you the same head rush as a sparkling new Walkman.

With all the unavoidable expenses you'll encounter, the most expandable/expendable portion of your budget will be your entertainment budget. Once you're through paying the various pipers who've threatened to cut off your phone, lights, or kneecaps, you will be spending your free time trying to make the pennies jingling at the bottom of your briefcase add up to McDonald's money.

There are several ways to make your "fun" money go farther. First, see if there's a book about free things to do in your city, and get hold of it. In New York, it's called *The Best Things in New York Are Free*. Most major cities have books of that genre. If your town doesn't, pick up a standard tourist's guidebook. Many have sections or listings of things to do that are not particularly expensive. Borrow one of these books (for FREE) from your local library, and make a list of those events that interest you.

Another good source of freebie ideas is your local "alternative" newspaper. Meant more for starving artists than for wealthy art collectors, these papers are usually conscious of their readers' desires to enrich their souls without impoverishing their change purses.

Many free events (including gallery openings and film screenings) can be very enjoyable on their own merits; add to that the satisfaction of having gotten something for nothing, and your evening's made.

If you have a VCR, try running film festivals in your apartment. An afternoon of Woody Allen or a Bette Davis bonanza, at $3 a tape, can come out to about $3 a person if you show three movies to a group. You pay for the flicks; ask a guest to bring popcorn.

If you prefer your drama live, see if any of the nonprofit theaters in your area need volunteer ushers. My cousin Amy and her roommate used to escort the paying customers to their seats at Washington's Arena Stage and Kreeger theaters once during each production. The symphony in Baltimore uses volunteer ushers as well. See what the options are where you live.

Finally, if you like your drama more raw than the latest Stoppard play, start hanging out in courtrooms. Many trials are open to the public, and they can be mesmerizing.

After sitting at any of these events with your eyes open and mouth shut, you may just want to get the jaws and teeth moving again. Zoom in on the "cheap eats" guide that will alert you to the haunts where a burger and salad cost less than a Monet original. The Zagat restaurant guides (they're available for several major cities) have a special listing of restaurants where you "can stuff your face for under $15." Eat moderately in any of these places, or at the joints coded with only one dollar sign in the back of magazine restaurant guides in local publications, and you're usually out the door on a ten-spot.

In general, Chinese food tends to be less costly than Western cuisines; learn to believe that Chow Fun *is* fun. Mexican food can usually be procured for poco pesos, as well—though what you save on dinner may be spent on Alka-Seltzer.

If you save in one area, you'll have money left over to pay for things you really care about. During my senior year of college, I scraped together the money to spend winter break in London. "Where is this money coming from?" asked my mother, who knew for damn sure where (whom) it *wasn't* coming from.

I told her it was my drug money. No, I wasn't dealing. With the cash I had saved by not blowing my senior internship salary on illegal substances, I and the companion of my choice (second choice, but Dustin Hoffman was busy that week) would treat ourselves to a week in Princess Di land.

"Just think," said my mother. "If you didn't *drink* either, you could travel to the Orient."

Now that I'm supporting myself, I'm drinking far less than I did at free-beer frat parties. Drinking club soda makes it easier for me to both buy clothes and fit into them.

In fact, my choice of linen blouses over liquor led me to devise the following money- and weight-saving plan. I like to think of it as being both penny- *and* pound-wise.

When I first started working, I bought chic new suits. Three months later, I couldn't zip them. With all the pasta I'd been eating to stay within my budget, I had grown out of my jeans. After six months of wondering why I was growing faster than my firm's client list while my co-workers stayed as small and bare-boned as our benefits package, I asked around and discovered that many of the slim staff members were hooked on the Bloomingdale's Diet. I tried it, but after a week on the Bloomie's Blubber Blitz, my waistline had shrunk not a whit. My wallet, though, suddenly fit into the pocket of my slinkiest slacks with nary a bulge. So I, who far prefer to spend my barely eked-out pennies on fashion than on foodstuffs, devised an antidote to the department store diet. Instead of spending my lunch hour eating, I shop. Spending neither money nor time on food allows me to (almost) close the new skirts I've bought, so that I have something to wear when I finally do go out to a nice restaurant.

12

1040 Is Not a CB Code

Keeping Records and Preparing Your Taxes

If your meals out are for business, you'll need to keep track of them for your taxes. My father, who has sifted through more people's tax records than even a serial murderer deserves to, promises that keeping accurate records will make your life (or your accountant's if you need one) far simpler come April.

My own records never seem to stick around long, as I've found myriad other uses for my receipts. Some people write thank-you notes on engraved stationery. I use canceled checks. My expense records are covered with grocery lists. I write letters on the backs of my cash machine receipts. A long-distance friend of mine recently received a missive that took up 1,632 of them. On the fronts of the sheets she learned about everything I've done in the past year. On the backs, she discovered which branch of Chemical Bank I withdrew money from on 12-10-87 at 11:53:29 P.M.

Last year, I took a phone message on the back of my W-2 slip. For a while, it looked as if the only call I'd be making was the one to my lawyer from tax-evaders' prison.

There has to be a better way. According to Bernie, there is. Take a large envelope, into which you put several smaller envelopes. This is the system those hand-painted nesting Russian dolls were based on. Label the smaller envelopes for the separate insertion of the following:

- W-2 slips
- Interest income
- Dividend income

These three will be empty until you get the forms for the preceding year each January. You'll also need envelopes for:

- Medical expenses
- Taxes
- Interest expenses
- Charity
- Miscellaneous deductions

Don't forgo this on the assumption that you won't have enough deductions to itemize. Wouldn't it be a shame if, in addition to spending three months in bed with a broken leg, you get stuck paying taxes on the money you used to pay the doctors' bills because you didn't bother saving them?

As you get the receipts in each category, file the slips. When your monthly bank reconciliation is complete, insert any canceled checks for deductions into their "homes."

Your bank reconciliations, like your tax records, should be current at all times. Even Arthur Andersen himself wouldn't be able to sort out your finances if your checking account is a mess.

When you receive your monthly statement from the

bank, compare the deposit amounts you've kept records of all month (haven't you?) with what the bank has recorded. If there's a discrepancy, call immediately (or next Tuesday, depending on whose favor the error is in). Before putting the checks in numerical order, compare them with your statement to see that all of your checks have been returned—hopefully without the words "insufficient funds" stamped across their bellies. Also make sure that the amount you've deducted from your balance for each check equals the computer magnetic-ink character-recognition numerals on the bottom of your canceled checks. Again, holler if the bank has made a mistake.

If your account gets so hopelessly screwed up that you can't do a reconciliation for six months running, close out the account and open a new one elsewhere. This is why most urban centers have banks on every corner.

Even when you do keep diligent records, April *is* the cruelest month. I won't go into the details of doing your taxes here, because by the time I explain it all they'll change the laws. (Death and taxes are both inescapable, but at least dying doesn't become more complicated every time Congress meets.)

If you suffer from insomnia, a quick review of IRS publication #17, *Your Federal Income Taxes,* will lull you to sleep with an up-to-date explanation of the taxability of your income and the deductibility of your expenses.

To further ease the pain of tax time, make sure you're withholding tax properly reflects your tax liability. Otherwise, you can discover at ten to midnight on the fifteenth that you have only moments to come up with three grand.

At some point, you may decide that you're spending more time preparing your taxes than you did earning the income. The more complicated your return is, the more likely you are to want an accountant to prepare it.

If a quick January run-through of your W-2 and deductible slips indicates that you won't be itemizing, and you don't own a home or have significant loan interest, and you make under $35,000 a year, it's pointless to engage an accountant.

If you're in the $35,000 to $50,000 range, you may want to use the tax services offered by many banks or by one of the national tax-return-preparation houses. If, in addition to being in this income bracket, you anticipate some degree of complexity in filing your return, you may want to consult a CPA.

When you're earning over $75,000 a year, you should definitely have your return prepared by a professional.

Do *not* look for your accountant in the Yellow Pages. Ask around and find someone who is active in professional activities and associations—someone whose credentials are more extensive than simple ownership of a green eyeshade and a number-two pencil.

Even if you are using an accountant, you'll want to keep accurate records. That man in the pinstripe suit has his meter running while he's sorting through your shoebox. Unless you're so successful that you're going to have a tax consultant on retainer, you'll want to do as much as you can on your own, rather than paying for the accountant to alphabetize your checks.

No matter how many professionals you can afford or choose to employ, your money is your own (well, the first three months go to the government, April's and May's paychecks belong to the student loan collectors, and the summer months' take-home gets turned over to your landlord. But the *rest* is yours!).

13

How the Tough Go Shopping

Shopping When the Economy's Tough

You've been saving your money diligently for a year now. Christmas Club, IRA, Grandson's Tuition Fund (you *do* think ahead!). Don't you feel great? Don't you feel virtuous? No, you don't. You feel lousy and deprived. You feel as if you've eaten every Brussels sprout on your plate, only to be sent to bed without dessert anyway. You want to splurge. To treat yourself. To shop till you drop.

Each respondent to my survey listed one thing they absolutely would not do without, no matter how broke they got. The answers range from the practical ("a good pair of boots") to the palatial ("my own house"). Other must-haves included manicures, fine wine, magazines, and beer. Some people refuse to live without the latest CD, while others spend their splurge money on Godiva chocolates. Personally, I can't stay away from books. Get me into a bookstore and I'll emerge an hour later, glassy-eyed and laden down with packages of books I'll never open, much less read. (Read? Who has time to read? I'm too busy shopping for books!)

Whatever your "reward," treat yourself occasionally. Otherwise you run the risk of the crash dieter; you'll be perfectly austere for a week, and on the eighth day, you'll gobble everything in sight. Only in this case, you'll pay not with a bellyache, but with a barrelful of bills.

In addition to the occasional splurge, you'll probably want to use your money for major purchases: a car, a television, a vacation. When doing so, shop around for a few weeks, but try not to make yourself crazy. No matter how little you pay for your stereo speakers, you'll see them at another store for $10 less the next week. The same is true for air fares.

If you'd like to get a terrific deal on a flight, consider flying as a courier. A company called Now Voyager, in New York City, can arrange for you to fly to cities all over Europe for a fraction of the retail ticket price. (You buy your own ticket to New York.) The only catch is that they can't guarantee to put your traveling companion on the same plane (in fact, they almost assuredly can't; he or she will have to fly over the next day). Also, you can take only carry-on luggage. Your storage space is sold to a company that has to ship goods across the Atlantic. Once in Europe, you can travel by Eurailpass—you can get a youth pass until you're twenty-six.

Most of us, though, will get no closer to Europe our first year out of school than we will to Neptune. More realistically speaking, then, here are ways to save money and take a trip you can afford and enjoy.

First, figure out where you have friends or relatives you

can stay with. Do you still have friends in the city where you attended college or grad school? Go crash with them, and do take advantage of all the local sights you were too busy for in your student days. Cheaper still: take a week's vacation and spend it as a tourist in your own city. Walk around, go to the museums, and send your friends tacky postcards. Bring a camera with you. Not only will this make you fit in with the folks from out of town, it also will encourage you to look more closely at things you usually take for granted. Eat in the tourist traps you usually wouldn't be caught dead in. Do not answer your phone. Do not open your mail. Do *not* give up after one day and spend your week watching "I Love Lucy" reruns. (If you want to watch TV call in sick, silly.)

Even with all the ways to save money on vacationing, most of my respondents listed travel as their most significant purchase since graduation. But there are other big splurges you may want to consider: Do you love art? Maybe all your months of hard saving can be traded in for a beautiful photograph or litho. Think of it as a treat, not an investment. The kind of art you can afford on a first-year salary will seldom turn out to be the profit-maker of the year. Buy what you *like;* if you want to profit, buy something ugly—like a T-bill.

Ditto for jewelry. Forget the Hope diamond, and buy something you'll enjoy wearing. Gold jewelry does not appreciate the way bullion does. Jewelry is a treat. Again, if you want an investment, forget the shiny stuff and go for the dull paper finish of a stock certificate.

There are a hundred more ways to spend your money, and you probably don't need me to suggest them. The best thing about spending your money (and investing it) is that you are accountable only to yourself. If you're broke, it's your fault. If you save money all month by eating only tuna (chunk, not solid, you thrift-o-maniac) and spend the balance on silk underwear, no one has to know (although if you've gone out and bought silk underwear, you're probably hoping *someone* will notice).

But be sure you're not spending money as a constant form of escape from life's problems—especially if one of those "problems" is impending personal bankruptcy. It's hard for those of us who grew up in the free-spending eighties to reign in our spending habits, but if you're careful not to waste money on things you don't really want, you're more likely to have a few dollars handy when your eye lands on the trinket you simply can't pass up.

14

Meeting and Greeting

Your Postcollegiate Social Life

For the first few months I was back in my native New York, my only new friend was the man who sold me my Sunday *Times*. "Heavier than usual today," he'd say, and I'd nod, satisfied that I had made my social effort for the month.

The fact that most of my friends were living within subway-hopping distance did not exactly motivate me to explore the vast and uncharted social terrain of my new neighborhood. Many of my summer-camp chums, high school buddies, and college companions had recongregated in the Big Apple as if drawn by a sale at Saks. I was going out three or four nights a week (which was that many times more than I could afford) and running up phone bills that would rival a bookie's. Thus, while I had no *new* friends, my old ones were just fine, thanks. I was pretty satisfied with my social life, and went months before making any effort to expand or update my social circle.

Making friends after you graduate is possible (and probably inevitable after a while), but the prospect can be daunting. In school, you have to make a concerted effort *not* to make friends; they don't call those four the "best years of your life" for nothing. Once you're out, though, meeting people actually takes some thought and—gasp—planning.

For decades, you've had friends handed to you on the silver platters of the playground and the poli-sci discussion section. After all that time, it's hard to approach friend finding as an "activity," or to actually think about how you're going to meet people. Many of us think friendship, like a good haircut, should fall right into place. *Scheming* to make friends? How early-eighties networking, we snort. How desperate! How depressing! As a result, many first-year Real Lifers spend their first few months complaining —but doing little else—about their lack of new friends.

Laziness is the prime obstacle to making new friends; but there are other factors at play that can predictably result in social stagnation.

"Many people are frightened of one another," says psychologist Tessa Albert Warschaw, Ph.D. "A lot of people haven't developed the social skills that allow them to take the necessary steps. You have to understand your own style. Some people forge into life. Others are more judgmental, and therefore more selective. Still others load themselves down with their friends and their friends' problems; anything outside that world frightens them. Then there are passive people. Everyone likes them, but still they're terrified of rejection."

And all of this makes sense. Who, after all, *isn't* concerned that at the end of school, the party's over? Who's so sure that the big city is just waiting to welcome him with open arms, or that in a matter of weeks, she'll be the toast of *tout le monde,* invited everywhere but the White House, and left off *that* list only to prevent the First Family's being overshadowed?

The best way to overcome those fears is to stare them straight in the face—and then ignore them. Sure, the first step can be the hardest, but once you start initiating new friendships, you'll begin to remember that you were a little nervous when *college* started, too, and that making friends at school actually proved to be easier than it looked on dorm move-in day.

So take heart: while the majority of the respondents to my survey listed their friends as the most-missed aspect of college and grad school, the majority have moved on and built new relationships with people they've met since graduation—people they've gotten to know at work, in their apartment complexes or neighborhoods, and through old friends.

You'll probably feel compelled to look for new friends more quickly if you move to a town where you have no *old* friends to depend on. Otherwise, you'll spend your first year sitting in your apartment crying your way through cases of Kleenex. When Lisa Belko married and moved to her husband's native Milwaukee, she arrived in town knowing no one but him. And he spent much of his time studying for his medical school classes. "It's really hard for me here," she said six months after the move. "Hal's friends from high school are around, but I don't know them that well. Anyway, I feel as if they're *his* friends, and I'm there just because I'm his wife. I guess it's going to take me a while to make friends."

When you're living away from your roots and are *totally*

on your own, things can be even harder. But for many, the fact that they can't rely on old friends in the new town provides the incentive necessary to get out and start meeting people. "I know that if I don't make the effort, no one's going to come looking for me," said a recent graduate who moved to Dallas alone.

Even if you are surrounded by your old friends, you may soon decide there is much to be said for getting out and meeting new people. Otherwise, it's easy to slip into a rut, and go through the days only half aware and only half enjoying the possibilities of your new life.

"Most people work on automatic pilot," says Dr. Warschaw. "They're not aware of what they're doing. First, you have to become aware. Ask yourself what you're doing. When you're in a rut, you feel it before you know it. You'll notice that you're going to the same restaurants, seeing the same people, telling the same jokes. You're not expressive in your relationships or actions."

This is exactly how I felt after a few months. Same bat life; same bat channel. How nice it would be, I finally thought, to order a gin and tonic without being reminded of what happened the time I drank seventeen of them freshman year. And wouldn't it be wonderful to meet people who didn't know the intimate details of my life's story, so that I could talk about new movies for a change, instead of rehashing old boyfriends?

If you're in a similar rut, Dr. Warschaw suggests you ask yourself some questions: What actions have I not taken that I could have? What clubs haven't I joined? Am I active in politics? What activities could I pursue that could be helpful to my career?

Letitia Baldrige suggests that you get into some new activities to broaden both your horizons and your social framework. Among the activities she encourages you to try are:

- Gallery tours
- Bird watching
- Film festivals
- Foreign affairs discussion groups
- Community theater or chorus groups
- Eating lunch in a park or plaza near your office

Another excellent way to meet new people is through charity work. Eleanor Raynolds, co-author of *Beyond Success: How Volunteer Service Can Help You Begin Making a Life Instead of Just a Living*, says that getting involved in a nonprofit organization is a terrific way to make new friends. "When you're working on something you believe in," she says, "you're bound to meet people with similar values. Volunteering is a great way to work side by side with people, and get to know them in a fashion you wouldn't at a cocktail party. You see how people react under stress and as a reaction to pleasure. You get to laugh and struggle together."

If you think you might want to get involved in a worthy cause, you must first decide what *you* consider worthy. "Ask yourself what bothers you," Raynolds says, "and get involved in an organization that tries to change that. Does illiteracy upset you? Join a group that fights it. Are you bothered by the way hospitals treat people? Maybe you should volunteer at a hospital."

Anyone I spoke to who has given their time to a charitable organization agrees with Ellie Raynolds: volunteering is a great way to extend your life beyond the constraints of the office.

Which isn't to say that the office itself isn't a wonderful place to make friends.

After *my* initial three months of social stagnation, I began extending myself to the most accessible group of potential new pals—my co-workers. Many of them became my close friends. We're still in touch, even though many of us have moved in different professional directions.

You're likely to find work is your greatest source of new friends, too, especially if you, as I did, work in an office where the average age is thirty-two (it would have been lower if the bookkeeper hadn't stayed past traditional retirement age).

Even in the friendliest offices, though, it's hard to jump the gap from polite acquaintanceship to bona fide friendship. Because professionalism is the order of the day, and those days are packed with clients to see and memos to write, initiating an office friendship can take some extra effort.

Letitia Baldrige suggests you invite your office peers to lunch one at a time, once a week, until you have had the opportunity to meet each of them. Don't be shy about extending the first invitation to take out lunch or take in an after-work movie with a co-worker. You'll find that, if nothing else, having friends in the office makes it a little easier to face Monday mornings. Many of my respondents who had expanded their circles beyond the group with which they went to school started with work friends. This is especially important in gargantuan cities like New York and Chicago, where it's easier to meet the guy at the next desk than the one in the next apartment building.

Unless there's anything going on in your life (drug smuggling, for example) that could be ruinous to your career if discovered, there's no reason to shut out your co-workers, or to keep things "strictly business" after hours. Drinks after work are a good way to know your colleagues as "real people," and to unwind after a seemingly endless day in the corporate salt mines.

This doesn't mean that *everyone* at work is destined to be your best friend. The CEO probably has other plans Saturday night. The woman who was passed over so that *you* could get a promotion probably feels no burning desire to throw you a surprise birthday party.

When you *do* socialize with office mates, try to avoid the temptation to gossip about your colleagues or speculate about which member of the cost analysis team has been sleeping with the night watchman. Stick to talking about new movies (or even rehashing old boyfriends/girlfriends!) and you'll find office friendships can develop into some of the more rewarding ones you'll enjoy.

It's only logical: Your co-workers share at least some of your interests, as well as a close approximation of your weekly schedule—compatibilities that facilitate plan making. What's more, they're as underpaid as you are, and thus won't insist on making every evening out a bank-breaking affair.

It's easy enough to make friends with your office mates if they're young and friendly. Unfortunately, not every office is a frat party just waiting to happen. While I was enjoying 9:00-to-5:00 (or 9:00-to-7:00 or -8:00) with my co-workers, some of my friends were toiling away in senior-citizen-populated work spaces where they alone were unable to remember the day Kennedy was shot. Others, who entered family businesses or small companies with few employees, also found it hard to make new friends.

My friend Gayle, for example, took a year after college to do pediatric asthma research, in preparation for (and to take a break before starting) medical school.

"I pretty much stuck to my old friends," says Gayle,

who, like me, was surrounded by friends from her earlier days. Her medical "subjects" were a bit young for a Friday night at the latest New York hot spots, and probably would have demonstrated an unfortunate tendency to wheeze through the best part of a movie. Most of the physicians and technicians with whom she worked left the hospital nightly for a spouse, a kid or two, and another evening of suburban bliss.

Gayle realized what a difference having peers at work makes when halfway through the year another young woman started working with her. "I got to be friends with her," Gayle says, "and having someone to give me that added 'umph,' I was more willing to venture out to other departments and make friends with some really nice people who I hadn't known were there all the time."

Naturally, it's easier to make friends when you aren't the only rookie in your office. In management training programs or law firms, the initiates who are thrown together (often seven to an office) and bound by their low-on-the-totem-pole status have half the battle of making office friends won.

If your job is *not* fertile ground for cultivating new friendships, though, or if you'd like to meet other interesting new people to hang out with, it may just be time to override your mother's oft-stated admonitions and start talking to strangers.

Mostly, you'll meet these "strangers" through people who *aren't*. If your best friend works with a group of recent grads while you're stuck in a three-person storefront, ask if you can tag along on your buddy's next informal office outing. While you may feel out of place at first, you'll get the chance to meet people you otherwise wouldn't. The office crew will probably welome the chance to meet *you*, too, and to talk about something other than the latest department crisis.

Another way to "share" friends with your existing cohorts: if you have old friends whose circles don't really overlap with yours anymore (high school friends, for example, who have developed whole new crops of amigos), suggest getting a group of "yours" and "theirs" together for lunch (if office locales permit) or for drinks on a weeknight. Again, your initiative is sure to be appreciated by all involved, and your circle will begin to widen. To paraphrase the old shampoo commercial, you'll make two friends and they'll make two friends, and so on . . . and so on. . . .

Right. How easy it is for me to encourage you to strike up a conversation with anyone who is remotely connected to you, or who sits next to you on the bus. The last time *I* spotted an interesting-looking (read: gorgeous) man on public transportation, I thought of telling him I liked his tie. I like his tie? Give me an A for effort, but a "back-to-the-drawing-board" for originality.

As I said, I *thought* of it. Unfortunately, socializing differs from gift giving in that the thought counts for nothing. Nada. Zippety-do. Mr. Necktie got off the bus having never heard my dulcet voice, and was thus deprived of the opportunity to ask for my phone number and use it to invite me to join him for a month-long trip to Italy.

By the time I got to work that morning, I was furious with myself. "I can't believe how stupid I am!" I shrieked to my office mate, who often had trouble herself believing how stupid I am. "If I did half the PR job on myself that I do for my clients, I'd have a date every night." (I know this because my friend Leslie, who *does* talk to people on the bus, does have a date every night. Well, almost.)

In public relations, my job was to talk to strangers, and

sell them on my clients. Shouldn't I be able to chat up a fellow bus passenger with the same aplomb as I would an editor? Am *I* not a more exciting topic of conversation than my client's antiacne gel? "Next time," I swore, "I'm going to speak up and 'go for it.' "

Try to avoid this Monday-morning quarterbacking. Unlike college, where "next time" will be Thursday at the library or next week at the calculus exam, "real people" pass much more quickly, like the proverbial ships in the night. If you want to meet someone, you can't wait for the right moment. The right moment is *now*, before he/she gets off the crosstown bus and meets someone more assertive on the downtown line.

There are several other standard PR lessons I've found useful in overcoming shyness. I learned many of these during my first year as a publicist, when I spent a large chunk of my time booking a media tour for a dermatologist who had just published a book. As you might imagine, Johnny Carson was less than interested in interviewing the author of *A Compendium of Complexion Concerns*. So were the hosts of most talk shows on air during the country's waking hours.

After booking Dr. Zit-Zapper in twelve media markets (which the less pretentious among you might call "cities"), I learned to accept rejection. I soon realized that, like most others, the PR game is one of numbers. If I called enough radio stations, *someone* would agree to interview my impetigo expert. Who cared, then, if nine newspapers' "Living Section" editors said they'd rather die; the tenth would interview my spokesperson, and that was all I needed.

I set a goal for myself of securing one TV interview, one print article, and three radio spots in each city. I just counted the ninety-nine verbal pink slips I received in between as the price for meeting my objective. I reasoned that it wasn't me they were rejecting, but the prospect of spending eight minutes discussing the difference between whiteheads and blackheads. I hardly cried once.

The abuse I suffered at the hands of the North American media toughened me to the prospect of rejection in my own life. So when, at my friend Michelle's Halloween party, I met a man who could actually walk, talk, and say "Booo," I pounced. Well, I didn't exactly pounce, but I didn't run and hide in the bathroom either. After the party, I asked Michelle for Keith's number, telling her I was going to (drum roll, please) ask him out.

She said, "You're really brave," which I'm used to hearing, living alone in New York City, "but what are you going to do if he says no?"

I reminded her that I had been turned down by no lesser men than Johnny Carson and Ted Koppel, and I forged ahead. Although Keith turned out to be even less interesting than a two-hundred-page book on skin disorders, I was one step closer to concluding that in private relations, as in public relations, faked confidence counts for almost as much as the real thing.

If I had called the local network and said, "You probably don't want to do an interview with my client . . . ," they probably wouldn't. If I made their decision for them (they're just going to say no anyway . . .), I'd have lost my opportunity and probably my job. But when I could fake the enthusiasm that—believe me—wasn't really there, and sound almost self-confident, my biggest problem was scheduling all the interviews into a too-short day. Similarly, if you get up the gumption to take risks in meeting people, you'll watch how quickly your efforts start to pay off.

Another lesson from Public Relations 101: Beyond the number of people you need to approach to make one friend, and the confidence you need to have—or fake—to approach them, it's important to develop those contacts that seem interested. When an editor sounds less than bored with your PR pitches, you ask her out to lunch—no sense losing a "live one." Similarly, if you've made initial steps toward friendship, you'll need to follow through. Call those three interesting people you met at that alumni meeting last week, and ask them to join you (and maybe each other) for a drink. If you get to talking with someone nice at a party, suggest getting together another time. Simple public relations.

I've reminded myself of these rules as impetus to strike up friendships with a woman with whom I got stuck on the subway home from a party, someone in a literature class I went to twice and then dropped because I had to work late so many nights that I never got to attend the sessions, and at least four of the strangers I interviewed for this book. When I'm in the right mood, it's simple. When I'm in the wrong mood, it simply doesn't happen. If it were *always* simple, I'd be out drinking psychedelic-colored margaritas right now, rather than hunched over my keyboard.

Nevertheless, there *is* a direct proportion between the number of social situations you force yourself into (and when you've been putting in sixty-hour workweeks, it *can* take force) and the amount of socializing you ultimately do.

My friend Sandy, who has been out of school long enough that people send her those birthday cards that kid about one's age, says she never believed she would make friends after school. Now, she has more friends than she ever imagined—people she's met at various jobs, on vacations, and in ballet classes; friends-of-friends, friends-of-friends-of-friends, and a few people she barely remembers *how* she met. "There is," she assures me, "life after graduation." I'm almost beginning to believe her.

15

I'll Have My Machine Call Your Machine

Finding Time for the Friends You've Found

With old *or* new friends, picking up the phone is hard enough; picking a date you and your friend are both free can be well-nigh impossible. You have late-night staff meetings on Mondays; he shoots hoops at the "Y" on Tuesday. Wednesday? No good; your mother has threatened that if you don't eat dinner with her, she'll submit your photo to the "Have you seen this missing child?" panel of the half-gallon milk cartons.

How's March? you ask. March is fine, says your buddy. You *do* mean March of '97? Or, wait, it looks like something might free up before then; is next Groundhog Day all right?

Without the proximity that throws new friends your way, faces from your past can start to fade like old newspaper clippings. Ask my friend Andi, whom I haven't called in three months. Or Stewart, my best friend from high school.

During our first year out of school, he lived three blocks away . . . and saw me exactly that number of times.

When you're working forty-five hours a week, spending ten more on the bus or freeway, and at least seven trying to find a shirt that doesn't need ironing, keeping up with your friends can be as tough as keeping secrets from them. My friend Jackie is an analyst in mergers and acquisitions. Given her crazy schedule, we're lucky if we merge once every eleven months to acquire a cup of coffee.

Cindy, another woman I saw every day at school, works in import-export. The only way I can see her is to have myself shipped to her office in a brown cardboard box, via Bangladesh.

Apparently, I'm not alone in facing this problem. "What's one thing you expected to happen since graduation that hasn't?" I asked in my questionnaire. "I thought I'd be able to maintain the close friendships I had in school," wrote one man who's living far away from most of his undergrad friends. ". . . I am in touch with some but not all of the people I considered 'close friends.' "

This phenomenon is sad, but not surprising. Just ask your parents how many school friends *they* still keep up with; the number's sure to be almost as depressing as the one in your paycheck column marked "net pay." Of course, correspondence is easier these days now that phones have taken the place of stationery. The discreetly used office WATS line has probably done more for the preservation of friendships than those mimeographed Christmas updates your Aunt Evelyn sends "from her house to yours."

But even when the phone call is free, using it to firm up social plans around two or more work schedules can be rough. If you'd like to talk to a friend and look at him at the same time, you're likely to find that the only way to spend time together is to run your errands in tandem on Saturday morning. It's amazing how much gossip you can catch up on in the pasta aisle of the supermarket, how fast you can reestablish personal ties while carrying neckties to the cleaner's. Waiting with a cohort on Motor Vehicles Bureau lines is a cozy way to spend a Saturday morning, too. The most social thing *I* did last week was wait with my ex-boyfriend in his ophthalmologist's office. (While I was there, I should have asked the eye doctor to check *mine.* What did I ever see in that guy, anyway?)

No matter how hard it is to schedule friend time, *do it.* "Your professional life is meaningless without a personal life" is the one thing New Orleans insurance saleswoman Emily Hicks has learned since graduation. Another respondent to my survey answered the same question by stating, "When you're so busy that you don't have time for your friends, it's time to sit down and do some serious thinking about your life."

Our generation cares more about our friendships—and less about making CEO—than our yuppie predecessors did. But even *with* an increased emphasis on the human factor, you've got to put some effort into translating your priorities into action.

So make seeing your friends a matter of priority, not a catch-you-whenever proposition. Just as I make lists on Monday mornings of which professional contacts I have to call each week, I "assign" myself at least one friend from the "God, I should call her" category each weekend, and set aside an hour to call and chat. My friends love me for it. Ma Bell adores me.

You may have to schedule these phone calls at odd hours (which are cheaper, anyway), especially to reach your friends who are still students. My friend Shana is in law school; it should be illegal how long we haven't seen each other. Gayle, out in medical school in Cleveland, is too busy cutting up cadavers to "cut up" on the phone. Their terminal inaccessibility is mitigated partially by fierce love but mostly by the prospect of free legal and medical advice a few years down the line.

As you discover the difficulty of keeping in touch with college friends, you'll find the list of 127 "best buddies for life" with whom you graduated will dwindle down till you can barely field a touch football team. The bright side is that once the social chaff has been separated from the wheat, you'll appreciate your close friends even more, and will often, I've heard tell, stay friends with them for life.

Difficult as keeping up old friendships can be, they're more than worth it. "There's nothing like an old friend," my grandmother used to say. The older I get, the "righter" she sounds. Your old friends understand you as no one else can. They know your history and your family, and can understand what's important to you and why. This is probably why it's an old friend who's first to get the phone call announcing, "We're engaged" . . . "It's a boy" . . . or "My mother died."

"It's really important to keep your old friends," says clinical psychologist Cheryl Fishbein, Ph.D. "If you have nothing to anchor you to the past when you're first starting out, you're going to be very lonely and scared." But Dr. Fishbein stresses that old friends are not only "useful" but valuable and enriching. "Often what happens," she says, "is that a friend moves away or changes her life and your paths drift. Your phone calls become less frequent. Still, when you do speak, that closeness is still there. When circumstances throw you back together, you can resume the level of friendship you once enjoyed. Some of these people become your closest friends again as years go by, so it really is important to keep the friendship up if it's meaningful to you."

Along these lines, you will discover that not every friendship proves meaningful. General rule of thumb: Anyone who wrote "Let's keep in touch" in your yearbook, won't. As a result, "I'll definitely call you soon for lunch" is the only lie uttered more frequently at alumni gatherings than "I love my job."

Speaking of alumni functions, they are the perfect place to see that second tier of friends you've been meaning to call since graduation—people you genuinely like but really don't have time for. You've let the phone call slip for six weeks, and now the sheer effort of lifting the receiver and pointing your dialing finger seems monumental. Reconnect over cheap wine underwritten by ye olde alma mater.

Friends who've moved outside the scope of your local alumni chapter pose another challenge: how do you make the transition from seeing someone every day to catching him for half a day on his way through town on a business trip? Last year, three of my close friends who had moved to the Midwest decided to come to New York for Christmas week. I had already planned to go away, though, so I caught them each for an hour in the airport lounge.

Given that my friends live in Cleveland, Minneapolis, and Chicago, it's unlikely I'll move closer to where any of them lives before winter is permanently abolished by an act of Congress. Therefore, I've learned to keep in touch over the miles.

If you're lucky enough to have a job that involves traveling, seeing out-of-town friends can be a little easier. The same job that's keeping you *away* from your out-of-town friends can, surprisingly, catapult you into their backyards

—at least for a few days. I was more than happy to escort my dermatologist spokesperson to Boston, during my first job, and happier still to charge dinner with my friend Elaine to his account.

Volunteering to represent your department at the Cleveland convention is a great way not only to see an old friend, but also to make plenty of new ones; the office mates you're relieving of this otherwise odious chore will love you for life. If your business trips take you to ports of call that are no closer to your friends than your own apartment is, hang on. Many companies allow employees to keep the bonus miles they earn as frequent fliers. Use these to visit your friends.

Now for the bad news: Your first year on the job will probably be spent *on* the job (imagine that!) and you probably won't get away much on business. And on a first-year salary, your hotel budget can probably be heard jingling at the bottom of your coat pocket. How nice that your friends' living rooms are free. For the price of air fare plus a bunch of flowers, you can spend a luxurious week on the floor of a friend's studio, drinking cheap wine and catching up on things. By the time you're up for vacation, your friends will probably be familiar enough with their hometowns to show you around. If this sounds any less appealing to you than seven days in an overcrowded Holiday Inn getting no tan because you could afford to get a room at the beach only in rainy November, you probably need new friends.

16

Isn't It Romantic?

Real Love Life 101

So much for being far from your friends. What about that girlfriend you left behind on campus? Or that guy you're crazy about, who's a crazy distance away? After living no farther from your girlfriend/boyfriend than the other side of campus, even a crosstown commute can seem like a long-distance relationship. If your valentine is living in the long-distance calling zone, you'll have a whole set of challenges to face and questions to answer.

First, can this relationship be saved? If you and Mr./Ms. Right will be apart all but three days a year, can you continue your relationship? Do you want to? "Most of the literature on commuting romances says 'Lots of luck,' " says Carole Wilk, Ph.D., a couples therapist. "When you're conducting a love affair over the telephone, you call each other for the big things—and to T-A-L-K. But it's the little things that get lost—the who-said-what-to-whom and guess-who-was-wearing-what-last-night chatter that keeps you close."

Sometimes, you miss the "big things," too. "When my grandmother died, he wasn't there," says one woman involved in a long-distance relationship. "We haven't spent a birthday together in two years," says a man whose girlfriend is still an undergraduate.

The chances of keeping your love alive long-distance are increased, says Dr. Cheryl Fishbein, a clinical psychologist, if there's an end in sight. "It's easier if you can say, 'We just have to put up with this for six months, or a year,' " she says, "than to go on with no resolution in sight. Either way, it's tough."

If you want to beat the odds, Dr. Wilk says, there's a key: "You've got to have an open, ongoing system of communication."

Given the problems of a long-distance relationship, you'd better be sure you're putting up with the phone bills for love, not security. A lot of people, Drs. Fishbein and Wilk assert, hang on to a no-win relationship—even one that's far away—because it's easier than looking for someone new.

Similarly, a lot of people hang on to in-town attachments long after they've reached their natural conclusion. "Two people who had everything in common in college may find they're out of sync after graduation," says Dr. Wilk. "If you're finding this is the case, try to let go—even though that can be tough."

All of my respondents agreed that meeting people to go out with is tough. But the data indicate that we haven't given up. Yet.

Each time a questionnaire came back in my mail, I

ripped the envelope open and turned to the question "What's the best way to meet people to date?" Each time, I hoped I would learn something new (for *myself;* the hell with research). Mostly, people told me what we all know: the best way to meet people is through friends, or in situations where everyone is relaxed and social. Specifically, people suggested the following:

"Blind dates."

"At work."

"At the beach."

"At other friends' small parties or gatherings."

"Community activities."

"A political campaign."

"Fate," said one man, and some of the stories I heard bear that out.

Myra Berg met one (now-defunct) boyfriend while she was looking for Mr. Goodbar. Sort of. Myra and her roommate were coming home from a bar late one night, and decided to stop into the video rental place and borrow the worst movie they could find. The salesman couldn't believe *anyone* would actually pay to see *Looking for Mr. Goodbar.* In fact, he was so shocked that he decided to call Myra the next day (her phone number was on her credit card slip) and find out what she had thought of the flick. Just as he had prayed, she hated it. And just as she hoped, he asked her out for a drink. It was the first of many over a several-month period.

Howard Koch met his girlfriend waiting on line at the trendy bar he "bounces" at. "She is definitely not the kind of girl to go to a place like that, but it was her friend's birthday," Howie explains. "And I'm surely not the kind of guy to work in a place like that . . . but it helps pay my rent. We met while she was on line." In addition to the fact that they were both out of place at the bar, the two have lots more in common, and the relationship is going very well, thanks.

Here's my all-time favorite "how we met" story. An elderly woman was brought into the hospital, in much pain and a bit disoriented. When she began crying out in Yiddish, the language of her childhood, none of the doctors could understand her. Except for one. He calmed her down. She was grateful. So grateful, in fact, that she whipped out photos of her granddaughter and told him to call. He did. They dated. They married. The granddaughter and her new husband moved out of her apartment and sublet it to me at a bargain rate.

Now *that* is what I call a happy ending.

Besides these fluky twists of fate, the best suggestion I received for meeting men/women was: "Be a student!"

The worst way, everyone agreed, is "at the bars." The only person who disagreed with this was Carol Klein. She met her boyfriend in—you guessed it—a bar. "We joke about it all the time," says Carol. "After all, who ever heard of someone really meeting someone in a bar?!"

Many of the young urban cowboys who are still looking for love in all the wrong places expressed disappointment with the state of their love lives. In fact, many of my respondents identified LOVE as the one thing they would have expected to happen to them by now that hasn't.

"I thought I'd have a serious girlfriend by now," wrote an actor in Philadelphia.

"I thought I'd know more women," says a marketing executive in L.A.

"I thought I'd meet someone special," a bank trainee said.

"I would have expected to be in a deep relationship with someone, not just superficial stuff."

I have reams of paper with these answers. Maybe I'll throw a party for everyone who answered the questionnaire and make a few matches. . . . Anyway, it was comforting to know that mine isn't the only door that's not being beaten down by the hordes of eligibles.

When I graduated and moved to New York, I felt luckier than a lottery winner, having a whole city of men at my feet. I soon learned that most of stuff "at your feet" in the city is the contribution of local dog walkers.

I wish I could say I had a date every night during my first year out of college: handsome bankers, older, wiser foreign correspondents, a bartender or two, and an old boyfriend back in town for one brief, beautiful weekend.

Failing that, I'd settle for the sympathy vote—the poor girl, let's buy a hundred more copies of her book and make her feel better—for claiming I had spent every Saturday night alone, organizing my pantyhose drawer by color and number of runs per pair.

Somewhere in between lies the truth about my first year as a s-i-n-g-l-e woman. Single. The same switch-the-tassel moment of graduation that catapulted me from cushy parental support to life with $23 in the bank also pushed me over the fine line between "not having a boyfriend right now" and being single. As in singles' bars, singles' parties, and Campbell's Soup for Singles.

I was not looking forward to this one bit, having heard singledom described as the only state worse than Rhode Island. I knew that things would not be made easier by my decision to enter public relations, a field so female-dominated that even the men's room attendants wear skirts. Women in other female-dominated professions, like teaching, and men in professional boys' clubs like engineering may encounter the same difficulties in meeting people, because even if you don't date your co-workers, your opposite-sex office mates might have cute friends. When your office looks like a sorority (or fraternity), this is less of an option.

When I announced to the world at large how hard I was finding it to meet men, suggestions for ways to meet guys poured in like sweepstakes entries. "Why don't you join the Vertical Club?" asked my aunt, referring to an expensive New York gym that, given the objective of most of its already perfect-bodied clientele, should be renamed the Horizontal Club. All kidding aside, I really *have* heard that gyms are good places to meet people and make friends. I even know one woman who met an adorable guy at the Nautilus center.

There was plenty of other advice, too: Why don't you go to synagogue? my mother's friend asked, leaving me confused as to whether she expected me to meet a man or just pray for one. In either case, I can't imagine a great future for myself with any man who's voluntarily awake at 8:00 on a Saturday morning. But if you like to attend church or synagogue anyway, try to pick one that has a young congregation. My friend Patsi married a guy she met on the communion line. (Maybe I should convert?)

"I've heard supermarkets are a great place to pick up guys," my friend Jessica said. This rumor, like the Bubble Yum/spider eggs gossip of our childhood, has yet to be proved. But in New Jersey, some of the grocery stores even have singles' nights. Pick up a woman while you pick up your white bread. That kind of thing. I'm very skeptical on this one. Every time *I'm* cruising the aisles, I find that the best-looking men are buying not pasta-salad-for-one, but Pampers for their one-year-olds.

Having struck out bending-and-stretching, kneeling-and-genuflecting, reaching for the Rice-A-Roni, I capitulated to the fix-up offers. Ultimately, it had to happen: the blind date.

The first of these gala evenings was arranged by my brother's girlfriend, who left me no doubt as to why she had chosen *her* beau (from a *fine* family) over the man she had described as "brilliant, good-looking, and fluent in several languages." Only too late did I realize that the same description exactly fit Mussolini.

Having arrived forty-five minutes late, Elliot quickly set out to make up for lost time, skipping right over the small talk and into the string of racist remarks he had prepared specially for the occasion. These exhausted, he began to regale me with tales of his grandfather's great wealth. I assumed this vast family fortune absolved me of any obligation to split the check, and after the waitress picked it up along with a much-too-small tip (how the rich get richer), I pleaded the need to get home immediately. Never mind that I hadn't been to bed before 7:30 since my mother levied a particularly cruel no-Brady-Bunch punishment in 1972.

Next up at bat was an attorney, described by my office mate as "a very sweet guy who's sick of the overly aggressive women in his firm." I quickly discovered that my eighty-seven-year-old Aunt Evelyn would have been deemed "overly aggressive" for Don the Dishrag. So would any woman who could breathe on a mirror and fog it up. After two interminable hours with him, I swore off blind dates "forever!"

"You have entirely the wrong attitude," says my sister, who was the blind-date queen in her single years. "You have to look at these evenings as a learning experience." I think she's been spending too much time with my mother.

"Think of it as a great way to network," she adds, naming people who've been offered jobs, cheap apartments, and introductions to the people they eventually married by less-than-exciting blind dates.

I've seen it happen, too. A few years ago, my friend Mitch blind-dated a woman named Beverly. She wasn't interested, but thought her co-worker, Sandy, might be. So she gave Mitch Sandy's number. No one's quite sure where Bev is these days, but Mitch and Sandy are home. Together. With their baby.

"It's not a question of how great a date is, but who the guy [or woman] knows," my sister says. "Also, lots of blind dates I've had have become some of my closest friends," she insists. Okay, let's say that out of twenty-nine guys, one's worth dating and two become friends. By my count, you've more than made your PR booking quota for the week—two print and a radio.

"So isn't it worth it," she says, "to make three lifelong friends even if you have to meet forty-three other disasters?"

You want to hear about disasters? Ask one hundred twentysomethings to tell you about "your worst date since graduation."

"My friend Sharon fixed me up on a blind date," one woman wrote in. "The guy picked me up at 8:00 P.M., and he knew I had just come home from a twelve-hour workday. We went to a bar (he picked it without my input), and when the waiter asked if we'd like any munchies, he said no, without asking me. That was bad enough. I figured I could eat at home, after he left. Only he wouldn't leave. When we got back to my apartment, he hung out for an hour, as I'm sitting there not only bored but about to faint from hunger. After about fifty minutes, without asking, he starts looking through my kitchen cabinets. 'Can I help you?' I asked.

'Yeah,' he says, 'do you have anything to eat around here?' " Despite this unpleasant experience, the woman who told this story still listed "blind dates" as the best way to meet men. Her worst? "Blind dates arranged by my friend Sharon."

The war stories continue:

"I finally got up the nerve to ask out a woman I had known for some time. She accepted quickly. Then she spent the whole evening telling me what a good friend I am. I mean, a really good *friend.*"

A date doesn't have to be blind for you to want to shut your eyes and have it over.

"The ex-boyfriend of the woman I was out with saw us together and attacked me. He had to be arrested for assault."

"My worst date was going holiday shopping with someone I was dating last December," says one person. "It was a disaster."

"I took my ex-girlfriend on a booze cruise," says another. "*Biiiig* boo-boo."

My own worst date was arranged by a neighbor of my aunt's. The guy was pleasant enough on the phone. More than pleasant, even: he was nice. I was very psyched for the date, not only because the guy seemed like a winner, but because I had just come back from vacation and looked tan and rested. My hair was just cut. I looked good, I felt good, I was up for a good time.

What I was not up for was a man in a polyester tie who hated everything I liked, liked everything I hated, and had no manners.

I ordered a glass of wine, which I placed to the right of my plate. The date from hell ordered a soda, which he placed *on* his plate, leaning over to sip from the straw (look, ma, no hands) each time he wanted more (I know, I know, it could have been worse. He could have started blowing bubbles). When it was time for the check, he snapped his fingers at the busboy. I wanted to break his knuckles.

It took him an hour to drive the two miles home, because he picked the busiest street in all of New York. I decided to make the best of the traffic by commenting on how beautiful the Christmas decorations made New York look. He retorted that he HATES Christmas. He HATES decorations. And he HATES New York.

Next topic.

"What kind of music do you like?" he asks. I name some Woodstock-era groups and a few of my favorite composers. He cites Minnie Pearl and the "Hee-Haw" crowd. A real country music fan. Well, hot damn. This was getting desperate. Finally, I remember he said he likes to cook. Figuring there was no way I was ever going to see this dude again, I opt for the Helpful Hints from Heloise, and ask if he has any good, unusual hors d'oeuvre recipes.

"My favorite canapé is cheddar cheese, cut into shapes with cookie cutters, perched on Melba toast," he says. I searched his face for signs of mirth. None. I had a Velveeta freak on my hands. Sensing my lack of enthusiasm for cheery-face cheddar sandwiches, he suggests something else: cream cheese. A hundred and one things you can do with cream cheese. Chive cream cheese. Rum-raisin cream cheese. Smoked salmon cream cheese.

Now, don't get me wrong . . . I have nothing against the folks that make cream cheese. I wouldn't dream of eating a bagel and lox without it. I even spent some of my happiest moments in the capital of brand-name cream cheese: Philadelphia. It's just that I don't think the white goop is the stuff that dream evenings are made of. Well, it turns out, neither does he. "What really makes a party festive," he says (and I thought it was cream cheese), "is those frilly toothpicks. The problem is, they're not that easy to find."

Neither, I guess, are well-dressed, sophisticated men whose favorite musical instrument is not the banjo. Help me, God. By this point in the conversation, we were still a day's journey from my apartment. Stumped for conversation, I look out the window, at people who look as if they're enjoying their evenings. I was quiet for a minute. Maybe three.

"So, are you always this ebullient," says Mr. Country Music on a Frilly Toothpick, "or is tonight a special occasion?"

When I got home, I kicked off my shoes and wondered what ever happened to that sweet guy from Wisconsin I dated a couple of times. (If you're out there, call me!) What ever happened to the jerk I dated in summer camp? (If you're out there, don't bother calling.) "I could have been home reading a good book," I moaned. "In fact, I'd rather have stayed home reading a bad book." This said, I swore off blind dates "forever." Again.

"Forever" rarely is, though, and I was soon back in circulation. (Nothing for the old self-esteem like comparing oneself to a dog-eared library book.) No question, there have been a few enjoyable evenings and Sunday afternoons, after which I didn't consider even for a moment taking out a contract on the person who had arranged them.

As I endure greater numbers of blind dates, I'm beginning to realize that there are ways to raise your odds of having a good time.

Do not, under any circumstances, spend a first date (blind or sighted) in a museum. You want to look at the paintings, but you know you should talk. But you really want to look at the paintings. But you know you should talk. So you end up making some incredibly intelligent comment about the paintings, like "Next to Monet, Jackson Pollock is my favorite Italian painter." And you wonder why this first date never turns into a second.

Your best bet is to go somewhere you can talk . . . first. If you go to a movie and *then* dinner, you'll spend the movie wondering what the hell you're going to talk about over dinner. When the conversation turns to the film, of course, you'll be speechless, having ignored the cinematic presentation to conjure up twenty-one witty things to say over dinner. Eat first. Try using a fork. Then, if you're both having a good time, you can do something else afterward.

After that particularly putrid evening spent in a restaurant an hour from my house, I voiced to a friend my philosophy that first-date dinners should be local. "That way," I reasoned, "if you're having a terrible time, you can get home right away."

"That way," my friend leered, "if you're having a *great* time, you can get home right away."

Of course, the best thing to be said about blind dates is that the worst encounters make the funniest stories. My friends and I have gotten each other through the worst rainy weekends with tales of our respective disappointments in the blind date department.

If you want to read about other people's misadventures (and triumphs) in the dating game, pick up a copy of *Tales from the Front,* by Laura Karesh and Cheryl Lavin (Dolphin/Doubleday). There are lots of horror stories, and lots of happy endings, too.

Horror stories notwithstanding, at least a few blind dates are inevitable—and, inevitably, a few are actually enjoyable.

"Even though he/she isn't someone I want to get involved with, I had a nice evening with a nice, new person." I've heard many dates described that way; it certainly sounds better than another night of "M*A*S*H" reruns.

If you are venturing out for a night on the town with a relative stranger, the vote is split on how to prepare yourself mentally for the evening. My own feeling was always "Expect nothing," until a friend commented that he could imagine nothing more deadly than spending time with a woman who was expecting to be disappointed. As time goes on, I'm learning to develop a cautious optimism. Because you never know what's going to happen.

Most people I know agree that the worst setups are ones initiated by distant family members. After all, do you really want to be stuck with someone who's compatible with the person you act like in front of Great-aunt Ida? Then, again, I know several married couples (including the one that bore and raised me) who were set up by Aunt Ida or one of her many, many sisters.

"Be wary of fix-ups by people who don't know you well" is another oft-quoted commandment. It makes sense. But then one of the most comfortable first dates of any kind I've had was with a guy who was given my number by a friend of my sister's. She had never laid eyes on me and knew nothing more about me than my age and college major. That things went downhill from there was surely not her fault (or mine, for that matter).

Much as I hate to agree with my sister (especially in print, whereafter she'll have proof), you really *do* have nothing to lose. If you've been given a number, use it; if you're called, go. There'll be plenty of time tomorrow to color-code your socks.

17

Not-So-Empty Nest

If You're Living with Your Parents

If you still have a key to your parents' front door, hold on to it: while the temptation to melt the old lock-opener down into a bogus bus token is great, so is the number of recent college graduates who end up moving back home these days. Because finding a job can take longer than it has in decades and because the cost of living goes up faster than many salaries, there are more twenty-five-year-olds living in the family digs than there have been since the days when the biggest danger in the big city was having someone step on your blue suede shoes.

If you think this is bad news for *you*, think about dear old dad and mom; they were just getting used to the fact that they could run around the house in their underwear, and have probably been anticipating the day they could stop housing and feeding you since the day you started kindergarten. Having to feed and listen to the stereo of a grouchy unemployed twenty-two-year-old isn't on anybody's Christmas list, believe me.

Besides the inconvenience of living with another generation (whichever side of the "gap" you're standing on), "returning to your parents' home can be a blow to your self-esteem," says Alice Juskowitz, Psy.D., a clinical psychologist, "especially when financial problems have already eroded your feelings of competency."

To make your return to the nest a little less stressful on everyone involved, Dr. Juskowitz suggests that you set a definite timetable for your stay. This could be either a number of months or "until I get enough money saved for the deposit on an apartment." In the latter case, she suggests, outline the steps you'll be taking to achieve that goal.

Clarifying your expectations will minimize stress for you and your parents alike. Besides discussing how long you'll be staying, make sure everyone in the household is clear about whether—and how much—you'll be contributing to household costs. If your parents decide to charge you rent, be sure to pay it on time. And look on the bright side: unlike "regular" landlords, parents recycle at least some of the money you pay them for housing into things like birthday and December-holiday presents. Start hinting broadly.

Also, determine the degree to which your lives are going to intersect and overlap. Will you be eating dinner with your parents? How often? Are you expected to show up at family functions you could get out of if you lived elsewhere? Parents are key examplars of the old adage "Out of sight, out of mind," and unfair as it may be, they're likely to expect a lot more familial participation from you than they do from your sister who lives in her own place across town. To avoid any hassles, discuss these issues *before* specific examples arise.

Also, discuss the household division of labor—how you'll

divide shopping, cooking, and cleaning chores. "Don't assume that the rules that applied when you were in high school are at work now," warns Dr. Juskowitz. "Remember that your parents also enjoyed *their* freedom when you were away in college. Respect their need for privacy and independence and they're more likely to respect yours. Your autonomy is best maintained by remembering that it *is* your parents' house, and that reviving adolescent conflicts will just make you feel like a teenager all over again."

To keep these conflicts at bay, Dr. Juskowitz suggests, try to conduct as much of your life as possible (especially dating and loud music-playing) outside the house. Get your own telephone line and answering machine. Keep reminding yourself that the setup is only temporary; it will be a lot easier to save your sanity while you save your pennies for an apartment of your own.

18

"One Rm, No Vu"

A Few Realities of Real Estate

Click your heels and say it three times: there's no place like home.

For four years of college, you moved into run-down places each September and out again in May, only to repeat the process on the muggiest day of the following autumn. You lost three socks, one sentimentally valuable piece of jewelry, and no small piece of your sanity each time. Now that you're graduating, you think you can move into a place that has your name on it for at least a full calendar year.

Not so fast. If you live in an overcrowded city, particularly on the East Coast, it just might be a while before you see your name on the door. Many of the apartments that recent graduates can afford are illegal sublets (I'm not advocating, just reporting). It's likely, then, that the name on your buzzer *won't* be yours, but that of the woman who lived there until her death in 1963. *Her* move out was probably followed by a string of fifteen under-the-table tenants, all paying more than the lease but less than the market value to the deceased's devoted (to his bank account) nephew.

New York is the capital of the illegal sublet. It was therefore a shock to many of my friends that my own name was on the front door of my first apartment.

"I'm so impressed with your place," said my friend Jodi the first time she came to visit. I glowed at the praise, having devoted more care to the decor than some do to brain surgery. "But it's nothing," I demurred, being commendably humble. "Really, it's just some stuff I put together."

Here she interrupted me.

"True, it doesn't look that great inside," said Jodi (ouch!!), "but you're the only person I know who actually has her name on her mailbox."

If you're considering an illegal sublet, consider, as well, that you're giving up not only your mailbox identity, but also all of your legal rights as a tenant. In short, if you choose to forge ahead with a forged lease, be advised that while time-worn tradition is on your side, the mayor and the landlord won't be. If you're found out, the landlord can toss you out like last night's leftover pizza. Then you're left out in the cold, alone with your collection of Hot Tuna albums.

Another thing about illegal sublets. They are (let's hear it for truth in advertising) *illegal;* I'd like to think that still bothers somebody. Of course, I'm not *personally* volunteering for this expensive brand of sainthood. If you know of a cheap lawbreaker one-bedroom in New York City, call me.

You probably won't sign a lease (legal or not) before you've done some serious pavement pounding. Before you even begin squinting at the classified ads, you need to decide where you're going to live, and whether you'll be dwelling alone or with roommates. The answers to both these questions may depend on money.

First, how much can you afford? Second: Is a place you can afford so far from your office that you'll need to show your passport on the bus home each evening? If you'd like to live in the center of the action, so to speak, you may have to pay more than you would living a bit farther off the main drag. In this case, one good way to cut rental expenses is to split them with a roommate or two.

19

Who's That in My Bathroom?

Finding—and Finding a Place with—Roommates

If you want to find a roommate, but don't have one picked out, there are several options. You could ask friends to spread the word that you're looking for an apartment mate, or you could advertise for one on a community bulletin board at your gym, church, or office. You can contact your school's alumni office, and ask them to put a notice in the next chapter bulletin. Or you can find your roommate where you found your apartment, in the classified ads.

My friend Michael actually found his first roommate by answering an ad in the *New York Times*. Despite my certainty that he would end up as the subject of a gruesome lead story in the *National Enquirer*, Mike's partnership worked out wonderfully.

After a year, the Parisian bank officer with whom Mike had shared a Brooklyn brownstone returned to his native

France, leaving behind the other half of the underpriced home (which has since been rented out to Michael's friend Ed) and a great recipe for crêpes Suzette. For Michael, living with a stranger proved a great way both to economize and to learn about another culture. If you think that you'd like to live with a visitor from a foreign country (maybe buff up your high school German?), check if local colleges have exchange students coming in for a year or two.

Even if you end up with (or prefer) the proverbial boy next door, the classifieds can be a good roommate hunting ground. Michael insists that he wouldn't hesitate to find another roommate through the paper if he were left with an empty half-apartment again.

There are also roomie-finding services that formalize, and claim to simplify, the classified hunting system. Check the Yellow Pages for such a service, and ask them if you can contact any pairs they've matched up for references. When Hank O'Hara's roommate moved out of the two-bedroom apartment they shared in a Los Angeles area complex, Hank enlisted the aid of such a service. "It's very much like a dating service," he says. "They have you fill out a form with your likes and dislikes, and put you through the computer. The service I used claims an 80 percent success rate. They charge $83 [1988 price]—which is a lot better than paying the other half of the rent by myself if I couldn't find someone on my own when Matt [his roommate] moved out."

Even when finding your roommate through a matchmaker, you should be careful: some strangers are stranger than others. Before you move in with someone you've never laid eyes on before, be absolutely certain you're comfortable with your unknown roommate's personality, safety factor, and economic stability. If you're the slightest bit wary about a prospective roommate's psychological, social, or financial state, hold out for someone more reassuring. Feel free to interview a prospective roommate as carefully as you would a doctor, or anyone else to whom you're entrusting your well-being.

Among the questions you ask, be sure to check partying and sleep habits. If 8:00 A.M. meetings are a regular part of your job, you probably don't want to live with someone whose idea of a good time is a 3:00 A.M. beerfest for seventy-five of his closest friends. Feel free, too, to ask for references, and check things out with the prospective roommate's previous apartment mates and/or employer. This will help you confirm that you're not about to move in with a loony, a deadbeat, or someone who lied about her employment on the computer form. (What else isn't she honest about? Your jewelry?)

When you're satisfied that your prospective roommate is no distant relative of the Boston Strangler, agree to have *both* your names on the lease. According to real estate attorney Jordan Metzger, if the apartment is rented in your name alone, and your roomie skips town, you could be paying two rents with one paycheck until you find a replacement. Also, Metzger says, if the lease is in your roommate's name and he moves out, you have no legal right to stay in the apartment. If the landlord wishes, he can kick you out to rent the place to someone else.

Similarly, if the apartment is legally your roommate's, you could return home from an eighteen-hour workday to find your boxes packed and his cousin Rodney from Rochester ensconced in what used to be "your" room.

If you're more comfortable living with someone you know than with a stranger, check around with friends of friends from school. Michael Olmstead, who graduated from the University of Wisconsin, moved to Chicago with two fellow alums he knew well enough to trust, but not so well that he was worried about ruining valuable friendships with arguments over whose turn it was to do the dishes.

"It's worked out really well," Michael says. "We respect each other's privacy because we were never that involved in each other's lives to begin with. When one of us hears of a party, he lets the others know. The fact that we have the bond of shared college acquaintances and experiences helps us all improve our social lives."

Another variation on the not-quite-a-friend-but-not-a-stranger-either theme is to hook up with someone you knew in childhood but lost track of until after graduation.

My friend Cindy spent her first year out of school living with Anne, a long-lost summer-camp friend. Anne's usually live-in boyfriend was away for nine months of graduate school, so she thought of Cindy and invited her to move in. Cindy, who had begun to panic about finding a place to live, moved her bed and bookcases into Anne's living room, splitting the rent and the space for what she knew would be a temporary stay.

Cindy knew that she could trust Anne to be a reliable and responsible roommate. On the other hand, they didn't know each other all that well. So they shared some activities, but basically they had their own, very different lives.

Cindy has recently lucked out again in the roommate-from-the-past sweepstakes. She is currently living in a huge two-bedroom co-op with Alison, with whom she carpooled to nursery school twenty years ago. "It's working out well," Cindy says. "She's even stopped stealing my Play-Doh."

If you'd like to live with someone whose *adult* habits you're more familiar with, you can hook up again with roommates from college, as Carol Klein did.

"The summer after college, I went to work in Italy for three months, doing research with a professor," Carol says. "When I left for Europe, I had absolutely no idea where I'd live when I got back. In fact, when I came *back* from Europe, I had no idea where I'd live when I got back. When I did get home, I called my college roommate, Joy, who is one of my best friends. She was living in Boston with her sister, and told me to come up there. I figured, Why not? and packed my stuff. It took me about a month to find a job, and Joy and I moved into our own apartment in the same building. It really made that first year easier, having the continuity of living with my old roommate again."

As appealing as living with an old friend can be, there is one danger: it's hard enough to force yourself to go out and make a new life during your first, scary, year out of school. When you're further insulated by the comfort of a live-in buddy, you're even more likely to veg out at home, rather than striking out on your own.

If you are moving in with an old friend, try not to rely *too* heavily on each other for social support, and don't expect things to be the same as they were on campus.

"When Margie and I moved in together," Abbie Konrad says, "I thought it would be like a fifth year of college. For a while, that was fine, but now either of us feels guilty if we make plans without the other; after all, we always used to do everything together, in big groups. It's hard to say 'Hey, I want to do this on my own,' without hurting each other's feelings."

There are still more ways to meet roommates and find a place to live. Hank O'Hara (our roommate service customer of a few pages back) had met his previous roommate, Matthew Harris, in the weight room of their apartment complex. Hank's *first* roommate was about to leave and Matthew was new in town, with only a one-month deal on the place he was in at the time. Because they each already lived in the complex, getting used to the place was no problem. Getting used to each other was easy enough, too, and both were sorry when Matt's office relocated and he had to move to the other side of L.A. Now he's living in a house with four other guys, one of whom he knew from high school and the others of whom he's met in California.

Still another avenue to explore: When Brad Lewison graduated from the University of Colorado, he moved to Washington, D.C., to work for his congressman. Because rents in the capital are sky-high and Brad's salary wasn't, he found another solution. For $200 a month, he lives in the local chapter of his college fraternity at one of the D.C. colleges. "It's a little rowdy," he says, "but you can't beat the deal. I'd be paying at least twice as much, maybe more, to live in such a nice part of town in a real apartment. Anyway, you can bet I'm never lonely with fifteen guys under the same roof." Many fraternities and sororities will rent out rooms to members of the national Greek letter organization if they have the space. Even if you don't see this as a long-term solution, it can provide a good stopgap while you're looking for a place of your own.

If you're looking to avoid the "rowdiness" of fifteen roommates, or the neurosis of one, consider living alone. I've lived by myself since my senior year at Penn, and have always been quite happy with that. After three years of maladjusted roommates, I was all too happy to adjust to living on my own. Not everyone feels this way, though, as I noticed in the local bookstore. There, nestled cozily on the shelf, between advice on *Making a Killing in the Stock Market* and a popular psychologist's affirmation that *Nice Girls*

Do!!, sits a volume whose title absolutely baffles me. Having lived alone through thirty-six rent checks, seventeen fights with the electric company, and one power failure (guess who lost the fights?), I find it hard to imagine anyone needing advice on *Living Alone and Loving It.*

Of course, I've found drawbacks to solo dwelling. For example, no matter what sort of complicated schedules I devise, it is always my turn to do the dishes. But it took me no time at all to adjust to the decadent delight of drinking milk straight from the carton. My more bizarre idiosyncrasies, previously repressed to accommodate the so-called "personalities" of my former roommates, are flourishing.

At last, I have arranged my spice jars in alphabetical order, as God surely intended. I reveled in the half-hour contemplation of whether to position Black Pepper between Bay Leaves and Cinnamon, or before Pickling Spice.

Finally, I can decorate my home according to my own tastes. No more "Jim Morrison Lives" posters. No more lava lamps. No more itsy-bitsy poodles, crafted out of cotton balls by a roommate's institutionalized mother. No more anyone else's anything. It's perfect. Almost.

The drawback is that living alone, one does incur additional expenses. I couldn't resist investing $7.95 for a Bob Marley and the Wailers album to keep me company. Whenever the quiet starts resounding in my ears, I crank up the stereo and wail with the Wailers in my best/worst Rastafarian accent.

If you think you'll enjoy the freedom to do that as much as I have, bear the following in mind:

- If you're living in a crime-ridden city, the bars on the windows are really worth the week's salary and the morning spent waiting for the locksmith who swore he'd show up by 8:30. Not because living alone is any more dangerous than sharing a home with three roommates and a Doberman pinscher, but because when you live alone, you'll imagine every pipe creaking is a crazy person, and every outside noise is the thundering approach of the next famous serial murderer. The bars, though ugly, provide great climbing tracks for your ivy. And your plants are sure to need all the help they can get now that they're relying on *your* remembering to water them.

- The three pounds of gourmet pasta salad you're tempted to buy, thinking you could make six dinners and three brown bag lunches out of it, will sit and rot in your refrigerator. Trust me. Buy only enough for one meal at a time. Repeated trips to the supermarket as you need things will up the odds that you're actually eating a vegetable in the same year it was harvested.
- If you want to get out, you'll need to make your own plans. No more tagging along with your roommate and his fiancée to Mexican dinners he pays for. When you have roommates, even a night spent in front of the TV seems like a party. Not so when you're watching alone. If you're the kind of person who likes to be busy every minute of the day, make plans in advance. Otherwise, you might discover that the quiet Saturday afternoons you used to enjoy are a little quieter—and a little longer—than you remember. Obviously, part of the reason for getting your own place is to enjoy these solitary moments. Just estimate in advance how many "moments" you want in any one-week stretch, and arrange for boredom busters in between.
- Accept the fact that from now on, it's you against the spiders in the tub. When you've got bug-bashing down pat, maybe you'd like to come on over'a my place and help me figure out what to do with the three mouseke-

teers who have made their home in my air-conditioner. Now that there's no one but you to deal with the apartment's flora and fauna, make friends with a good exterminator. Fast. Like the pizza delivery man's, his phone number will be committed to your memory in no time.

- About those delivery men. . . . Don't get *too* friendly. Start ordering out for food to eat alone in your apartment today, and they'll find you in six months, passed out in a paper plate full of chop suey, anchovy pizza, and Chicken Delight. If you're not hungry enough to put on sweatpants and pick the food up yourself, you're not that hungry.
- Pay the rent on time. When you share a space, you can always tell the landlord that your roommate, who pays half the rent, has skipped town to bargain-hunt in a shopping mall in Brazil. When the apartment is solely yours, though, any negligence in payment can and will be held against you. And if you're thrown into jail, odds are more than even you'll be back to living with a roommate.

So, are you going to live alone or with roommates? Before you start looking for a place, figure out how many people will be sharing your new "quarters" or, if the place is *really* small, "eighths." Come up with a collective budget, and start looking. With three of you scanning the papers and the apartments listed there, you can accomplish your goal faster. Take turns checking out apartments as you hear about them, and arrange for a committee investigation only after each apartment has passed its first inspection. Soon enough (or maybe not quite soon enough), you'll find a place you can all agree on.

20

Will You Be, Won't You Be, My Neighbor

Picking Your Part of Town

When you *are* ready to start looking for an apartment, expect to do some legwork. If you're undecided as to which neighborhood is best for you, scan the ads first for those neighborhoods that seem to have lots of apartments in your price range. This provides not only the obvious benefit of multiple options, but the greatest likelihood that the general cost of living will be within your reach. If most of the neighborhood's one bedrooms run at three times your budget, chances are the restaurants and dry cleaners in the area will be keyed to your better-heeled neighbors.

On the other hand, if many of the apartments in a ten-block radius are going for $53 a month, you're probably dealing with a neighborhood that's still in whatever war-torn phase of gentrification precedes "up and coming."

A realtor's saying, "It's an up-and-coming neighborhood" is a real red flag, and often means you'll be spending the six years before it "up-'n'-comes" locked in your apartment, afraid to go out after dark. Describing one such neighborhood, my real estate broker said, "If you rent now, before it starts going co-op, you can sneak in on the ground floor."

"If I rent now," I countered, "I'll be shot by a prowler who snuck in on the ground floor."

A bargain's no bargain if you have to pay $850 a month for a security escort. To gauge the safety of your prospective neighborhood, *don't* check it out on Sunday morning. Those twenty-seven other pedestrians on the block aren't locals who'll keep your street well populated and safe once you're a resident. They're apartment hunters like you, who will move in and become couch potatoes, leaving only you and the crack dealers on the street after 7:00 P.M.

If you think you're interested in a certain neighborhood, get to know it in more telling circumstances: ask a (big, strong) friend to walk around with you one night. If you're still comfortable, try it alone some night before you move in for good. After you've lived on a bucolic campus or in the suburbs, the city can be daunting at first. But don't feel silly if you're holding out for a really safe block. Better to feel a little bit silly than a little bit mugged.

Once you've found a couple of neighborhoods that fill your own safety requirements (and it really is a personal gauge), consider distance.

Bottom line: How long will it take you to get to work, and how far are you willing to travel?

When I was trying to find a new home, several well-meaning relatives (read: busybodies) suggested that I get a place in Brooklyn, where the rents are half those in Manhattan. It seemed silly, though, to commute forty-five minutes each day and pay $500 a month rent when I could live with my parents, only half an hour away, for free. So I ignored my relatives (what else is new?) and moved into town, only to discover that it would take me *fifty* minutes to get from my Manhattan apartment to my office by public transportation.

The difference, though, is that while my city's poorly planned public transportation system makes my neighborhood somewhat inaccessible, my apartment is an easy walk from almost anyplace in town. Thus, the fifty-minute-by-bus distance from my subway-unaccessible home to my office takes only an hour by Reebok—as compared with a two-day hike over the Brooklyn Bridge. Unless the weather was abominable, I could walk to work and burn off my breakfast-muffin calories before biting into my day's office agenda. Furthermore, on those "what-a-day" evenings when I wanted to be home in fifteen minutes, I could do it with a $5 cab ride, while taxi fare from the outerlying boroughs can cost as much as a swanky dinner and movie. If you're sacrificing the fresh air of the suburbs, you might as well live somewhere to which emergency cab fare home isn't going to break the bank.

As for living in the suburbs, that's becoming a more popular option as city rents skyrocket and developers start building apartments within reasonable commuter distance. Though I'm a city nut, my friends who are happy in the suburbs think I'm crazy to put up with the filth and prices in the city.

The city mouse/country mouse distinction is as old as the eponymous (eponymouse?) children's story. Most suburbanites I know would rather die than give up the smell of pine needles that wafts through their open (barless) windows, while the city folk wouldn't dream of living anywhere that isn't paved and pulsating. "You really should come out here one weekend," one correspondent told me of her tree-lined neighborhood outside the city. "It's paradise. We even have supermarkets. *Real* supermarkets, where they play Muzak in the aisles." After living in Manhattan for four years, she's willing to put up with redigested Burt Bacharach music to have more than one brand of spaghetti to choose from and that tree-lined street to carry it home through.

In many suburban areas (and in Los Angeles, often described as the biggest suburb on earth), though, you'll need wheels to get to the grocery store and to work and social functions downtown. Be sure to figure the cost of buying and running the car into your assessment of how affordable these suburbs are.

Think hard before picking your neighborhood; you'll be stuck there for at least a year, and if you're unhappy, it will seem twice that long. If you are moving to paradise in the suburbs, find an area that's full of young singles (or married people, if you are married yourself).

Louise Silverman, a relocation counselor for employees at several Fortune 500 companies, spends her days trying to help transferred employees find the right neighborhood in the metropolitan areas to which they've been moved. She has several tips for finding the right place to set down *your* roots.

"If you've taken a job in a new city, the first thing you should do is network and get in touch with people that live there," she says. "Maybe there's someone who graduated from your college and moved there last year . . . or the friend of a friend. Get information on the area from the Chamber of Commerce. Contact a reputable real estate agent. The agent shouldn't be looking to rent or sell you a specific place, but rather to help you narrow down your options in terms of which neighborhood to pick. Finally, you should visit the city yourself and look around." Pick up a copy of John Tepper Marlin's *Cities of Opportunity* (MasterMedia) for a rundown on the country's major metropolitan areas.

If you've signed up with a huge company, they may send you to an outside consultant like Mrs. Silverman. If not, many national real estate companies have affiliated relocation counseling services. Either way, the relocation counselor will take you on an area tour to give you an idea of what the town or city is like. If you're looking on your own, check out the transportation, the cultural life, the suitability of the neighborhood to your lifestyle and budget, and the security. If you have any questions, contact the human resources person at your new place of employment. He or she can put you in touch with young people who work at the company and they, in turn, can steer you toward the neighborhoods or suburbs that are good for young professional people.

Once you've found a neighborhood that's convenient and affordable, try to determine if you'll actually enjoy living there. Where are the movie theaters, the restaurants, the bars? How's the shopping?

When I first moved into Manhattan, my mother surveyed the boutiques and greengrocers lining the block and told me I was smart to move somewhere with such great shopping. A month later, *New York* magazine listed my corner as the best place to buy crack in New York City. I cut the article out and sent it to Mom, with "You were right about the shopping here" scrawled across the top in crayon.

What about your friends? If you're not moving into a

building or complex that's full of friendly people eager to meet you, you should try to live in the same neighborhood as at least one person you know and can depend on. If my friend Lynn didn't live around the corner, I would have had to sleep in my apartment the night I discovered a mouse under my bed at 1:15 A.M. But before you could sing "See how they run," I was sound asleep on her couch, thankful for friendly neighbors.

What kind of people live in your prospective neighborhood? Are you likely to meet anyone exciting in the laundromat, or are the local stores filled with forty-year-old couples? Many city neighborhoods, like Chicago's Lincoln Park, Dallas's Lakewood, Virginia Highlands in Atlanta, Cambridge and Somerville, Massachusetts, are veritable meccas for the young and the restless.

"It's great!" says my friend Craig of his Lincoln Park location. "Everyone's between twenty and thirty, and everybody's friendly. When it's nice out, the entire neighborhood hangs out in the park getting tan and playing Frisbee. It's incredibly easy to meet people in a place like that, because everyone else wants to meet people."

21

Be It Ever So Humble

The Apartment Itself

Once you've found a neighborhood, you can start looking for a place to hang your hat. And your coat. And the 37 shirts, 34 pairs of trousers, 13 dresses, or 145 neckties you've amassed in the five years since you stopped growing. In short, think closets.

"This place has great closet space," my mother said on first inspection of the apartment I was considering.

"No, Mom, this is the living room."

So much for closets; determine what other amenities are crucial to you before you set out to find an apartment. For example, how important is it to you (or to your parents, if they're a consideration) that you live in a building with a doorman? I have friends who moved into places where the security guard was glued to the door. So glued, in fact, that he couldn't be bothered phoning up to see if the three men with a mover's truck and sawed-off shotguns were expected guests. Depending on the city and the apartment setup, security could/should include human or electronic sentries, as well as parking lot surveillance.

As careful as you are in selecting a place, you'll inevitably have to make a few compromises. In selecting my first apartment, I thought it was more important to me to have a spanking-new place than to have lots of room. Three months later, the newly renovated saltbox had that "lived in" look I had wanted to avoid. Meanwhile, my place got smaller every day. For a year, I watered the apartment daily, hoping it would grow. The apartments across the hall in that same building are bigger and lighter, but they cost $35 a month more. While that doesn't sound like much, it's $500 a year—$500 I'd rather spend on a mid-February flight to a land where the word "slush" has never been heard.

Accept the fact that there are few perfect apartments, then, and (you thought we'd never get there) start looking through the paper.

Be warned that the print on the real estate pages is as small as the stock market reportage. The problem is, unlike the market, the rental figures only rise each week. And, unlike stocks, a studio never splits two for one to leave you with an unexpected bedroom.

For three weeks, I scanned the paper, identifying the least outlandishly priced abodes. I marked them in highlighter ink, finally using up the pens I'd bought to circle the "meaningful" passages of my Shakespearean comedies in my previous, rent-free life.

After spending a month of Sundays perusing the "apts fr rnt" ads, I was fluent in the lingo. Here's a basic primer:

Charming—small.
Cozy—smaller still.
Prewar—small and old.
Lots of character—lots of chipped paint.
Southern exposure—you can see across the alleyway to the apartment of the aging New Orleans belle in the next building. Depending on your taste, this might be worth a few extra bucks a month.
Newly renovated—pray that your neighbors have interesting lives, because you'll be able to hear every word through the spit-and-tissue-paper construction that's used to change small-and-old apartments to smaller-and-newer ones.
Junior four—your cousin Junior, who is four, is the only one who could fit in the spare room.
A steal!!—last tenant was robbed four times.
A must-see—if you didn't view it with your own eyes, you wouldn't believe they could ask so much for so little.

Understanding these terms will help you develop realistic expectations, whether you get an apartment directly through the landlord or use a broker. At some large apartment complexes, like the one Hank and Matt lived in, you can show up on the manager's doorstep and rent a place, often on a month-to-month basis. If your time is scarce, though, a broker may be a good resource.

Often, brokers charge a percentage of the first year's rent as a finder's fee. In my own experience, though, it proved worth it. After three weeks of driving into the city at 8:00 A.M. each Sunday morning to view the "no fee" apartments, only to find that there was not only no fee, but no apartment, I decided to enlist the aid of a broker. If you're considering this step, know the pros and cons.

On the plus side, you can be sure that unlike landlords with only one apartment to unload, your broker will show you several apartments, and will keep calling you with new openings until you've found a home. After all, he or she doesn't see a dime until you've signed a lease.

Because the broker is paid only when you sign, and because he or she is paid on commission, be prepared for the hardest sell you've encountered since the neighborhood bully tried to unload his '73 Dodge Dart on you. Most brokers will try to convince you that you can afford more than you are really able. They'll try anything, including laughing in your face when you state your original budget; telling you, in front of your mother, that the apartments in your price range are not as safe as the buildings in the higher brackets, and showing you three of the ugliest homes you've ever seen in a row, followed by one dazzler that runs $50 more a month.

"See what an extra $50 a month will get you?" coos the broker, and before you know it, "broker" has a new meaning: you've never been broker in your life.

If you are subletting a co-op apartment, you have a good shot at negotiating your rent down. With apartments impossible to sell these days, many owners are satisfied to recoup their mortgage costs. This is one of the few ways the recession can actually work in your favor!

In cities with tight rental markets, you may be desperate enough for a place to use a broker. If you have the stick-to-it-iveness required to stay within your allowance despite the viselike pressure of an apartment pusher, a broker can save you a lot of time.

Some brokers have holdings all over the city; these are

your best bet if you have an open mind as to what neighborhoods you'll live in, and want to see the most apartments possible. Other brokers specialize in specific areas. If you're sure you want to live in a certain section of town, using one of these brokers can up your options within that neighborhood.

Whatever kind of broker you use, he or she will ask you to register with them first, and sign a commitment not to rent an apartment they've shown you without paying their fee. This prevents your sneaking behind their back to the landlord and signing a no-fee lease.

Before your broker shows you any apartments, he or she will ask who you are, what you do, and how much you make. If the answer to any of these questions is unsatisfactory, you'll need a co-signer. Try to convince your parents to put their names on the dotted lines for you; this doesn't mean you expect they'll have to bail you out, but it will sway the landlord in your favor. In addition to providing your broker or landlord with information you wouldn't give your closest friend, you will also have to part with one or all of the following: a fee, first and last months' rent, and/or one month's security. If you're moving someplace with on-site parking, there may be a monthly charge for housing your car, and there might also be a security deposit or several months' parking fees required up front. Before you move anywhere, check into the total costs involved. It's usually greater than the simple rent and utilities package.

22

You Must Tell Me Who Your Decorator Isn't

Furnishing Your Place

Moving into an apartment, you'll discover, can be very costly. That leaves you with an apartment, but no cash left over to decorate with.

What can you beg, borrow, or steal from friends and family? Or would you prefer (and do you have the means) to start from scratch and buy all your own new things? Either way, you will certainly need something to sleep on.

Invest in the best bed you can afford. A lousy mattress will affect your sleep and, in turn, your cheerfulness in waking hours. If you're living in a studio, you might want to consider a good sofa bed or futon. My friend Andrea swears by her futon mattress because it rolls up and away into almost no space at all—leaving the decks clear for all forms of Jane Fonda workouts or at-home jazzercize routines.

Once you've taken care of your bedding needs, you'll also want something to eat on and something to sit on while doing same. If you're agile, your lap and the floor, respectively, can do for a while. Before the furniture's in, you'll have to stick to finger food, like pizza. . . . But who are we kidding? That's probably what we'd eat even if we had mahogany dining tables with sets of twelve chairs. My apartment is fully furnished and I *still* eat on the floor half the time. Part of the thrill of being on my own is that no one tells me not to. You may also want someplace for your too-old-to-sit-on-the-floor mother to park herself when she comes for a visit. If you're looking to discourage these visits, a lack of furniture may be just what you want. Otherwise, director's chairs are cheap, if a bit seventies. I don't care; I love them anyway. Besides being cheap, they fold up when not in use. If you saw how small my first apartment was, you'd appreciate the importance of that.

Outdoor furniture is another cheap and sturdy option. A lot of this tubular metal or plastic furniture comes in wild (or paintable) colors. Depending on the look you're after, they may offer the ideal combination of low price and high visual voltage.

Linda Jones, marketing communications consultant for Masco Home Furnishings, the world's largest home furnishings conglomerate, offers the following advice on beginning to furnish your first home or apartment after you graduate.

"Finding the best quality for your money should be your foremost concern when furnishing your apartment. Quality construction and durability are available at affordable prices; you simply have to know how to find them.

"For instance, comfortable seating is a priority, and fine construction and comfort go hand-in-hand. Sit in chairs at the store. Make sure they are level, the frames are sturdy, and there is not excess glue or finish on the exterior. Also, upholstery fabric should fit snugly, but be padded enough so that springs and the frame cannot be felt when you're seated. Remember, especially if you're in a studio apartment, you and your guests will be spending a majority of your time in the chairs you choose. You might even eat in these chairs frequently, so seating with stain- and spill-resistant fabrics is an intelligent investment.

"Today, there is a wealth of affordable, high-quality furniture available in department and specialty stores nationwide. Keep in mind, too, that you don't change your furnishings as easily or as often as you change your wardrobe, so really love the pieces you purchase—whether it's your first table or an entertainment center. Be willing to spend a few extra dollars if you find a piece you'd like to keep for a long time.

"Even though over time your taste will surely change, many different styles may be used together to express your personality. If you're really unsure of your style, it's always safe to invest in fairly traditional furniture and test your taste with very special accessories."

What else do you need? Do you like to entertain? You'll need enough chairs for your guests, and a table to feed them at. Do you expect a lot of friends to crash at your place on journeys through town? You might want to invest in a mini-futon or a spare mattress. Inflatable air mattresses can actually be quite comfortable and fold up to half a cubic foot when not in use.

Are you a big TV watcher? What are you going to rest your set on? Where's your stereo going? Where are you going to put your books? What are your other storage needs?

Once you have an idea of what you need, measure your apartment and try to plan out where everything's going to go. Nothing can be worse than moving twenty-seven pieces of furniture from your mom's house in Atlanta to discover that only fifteen of them fit into your new apartment.

If you're shopping for new furniture, the salespeople will often offer to help you conceptualize layouts if you provide them with a graph-paper plan of the apartment. Take advantage of their time and expertise, but be careful you don't end up living in someone *else*'s ideal apartment. Ultimately, this is *your* home (finally!!) and *you* have to be happy with the way it looks.

"Furniture is an expression of the person you are when you buy it," says Nancy High, director of communications for the Furniture Information Council. "Buy what's going to make you happy and reflect your lifestyle today, and don't worry that you're getting married to your furniture. If you don't have or want to spend the money to purchase a whole roomful of furniture, buy one piece you really like, and blend it with pieces you've borrowed or salvaged. As time goes by, you will get a better sense of your own style. At that point, you can buy more furniture—either in the same style as your first piece, or with a different feeling, to reflect your own changing values and tastes and to give you the look you're after."

"The best way to decide what look you're after," says interior designer Marion Auspitz, "is to look through a lot of decorating magazines. Cut out all the pictures that appeal to you, and then review the stack of photos. You should see certain trends emerging: Is everything you've selected very modern? romantic? country-style? Once you have a better handle on your own taste, you can work on achieving that style in the least expensive way possible."

Auspitz's strongest recommendation for getting rich looks on a tight budget is to put a length of fabric in one hand, and a staple gun in the other. "There are tons of things you can do to make a place over with fabric," she says. For example, you can buy a few yards (remnants are cheapest) and use the fabric to cover a beat-up old table. A flowery pattern draped over a round table can give the room a Victorian feel. Bright solids can give the room some verve without the cost of painting all the walls. Even if you're a spaz at the sewing machine, you can probably figure out how to make curtains for a lot less than they'd cost ready-made. Ditto for a duvet cover that can turn your ugly, avocado-green blanket into part of a chic new bedroom.

To illustrate what can be accomplished on the cheap with a little imagination and some planning, Auspitz told me how her nephew decorated his place. First, he painted the walls white. Simple. He bought lawn furniture, and painted it black. Carrying the black-and-white theme further, he bought some fabric striped in those colors and used it to cover a couch (staple gun and needle in hand) that in its previous life was an ugly brown print.

The next project was to take enough fabric in a black/white check to glue a strip around the circumference of the wall about two-thirds of the way up. Not only did this add pattern to the white expanses without the cost or labor of wallpapering, it also provided the ideal hiding spot for stereo and phone electric cords. To add some color interest, there are prints on the walls that combine the black/white color scheme with primary colors.

"It didn't cost him a lot," says his proud aunt, "but the apartment looks great. He found a look he liked, he stuck with it, and he used his own creativity to make the place stand out."

If you're living with two or three roommates, each of you bringing three mismatched-to-begin-with pieces from your respective parents, it's going to be harder to create a cohesive, polished look.

You'll notice that the cover photos on *House Beautiful* are rarely identified as "the spare yet elegant apartment of Mark Mitman, Andrew Polletti, and Gus Black, three recent graduates of Cornell University sharing a run-down two-bedroom in St. Louis."

As any newlyweds can tell you, it's difficult enough to merge styles and furnishing when you're in *love* with your new apartment mate. When you're practically strangers, aesthetic harmony can be even harder to achieve.

"Our place has sort of a temporary look to it," says Gregg Pfizer, of the apartment he shares with two other guys. "I guess if I had my own apartment, I'd pay more attention to how it looked, and make it a little more like a real home."

If you and your roommates plan carefully, you *can* make your place look a little less like a Hooverville Habitat and a bit more homey. Determine beforehand who'll be supplying what. Discuss which pieces you absolutely refuse to live with, and agree on a reimbursement plan in case Aunt Maggie's table gets ruined.

Catherine Crane, author of *What Do You Say to a Naked Room,* says that the best way to cope with roommate-participatory decorating is to discuss ahead of time what each of you likes and expects to do in your new home. You're going to have a problem, she says, if one roommate thinks the living room is for formal dinner parties, and the other thinks it's his place to leave dirty socks and gym equipment. It's also important, Crane notes, to design the apartment so that each of the inhabitants has private space. Arrange the furniture so that you're not all always staring at each other and, if necessary, erect dividers or hang curtains to give each of you a sense of having a room of your own. At the very least, agree who has dibs on spending time alone in which rooms, when.

If you and your roommates are pooling funds for new furnishings or utensils, write down *now* who keeps what when you split up. Rather than all chipping in and each owning one arm of the sofa, it's probably better to calculate what your total expenditures will be, and divide them by piece. Thus, one of you will own the couch, another will have claim to the TV, and a third will have possession of the pots and dishes. This will make life a lot easier when you split up and go your separate ways. (Just ask a divorce lawyer who's bought her third Porsche with the money she earned divvying up other people's loot.)

If you're living alone, you have the luxury of furnishing exactly to your taste. Without roommates to blame for the ugly pieces, you'll probably pay a fair amount of attention (and cash) to the ambience of your new apartment. The money and time you spend will be well worth it, I think. As much as you may insist that furniture and decor aren't important to you, it's hard to feel as if you're living a Real Life when your possessions are stacked in milk crates pilfered from the back of a supermarket and you're eating, standing up, off the plate you stole from the college cafeteria freshman year.

"Having your own furniture says, 'I want to tell you about who I am,' " says Nancy High. "In research we've done, the Furniture Information Council has found that a lot of people are frightened of this, and shy away from buying furniture for that reason. But by not making a decision, or not making a statement, you *are* saying something. You're saying, 'I don't care.' Even on a budget, you can make a few improvements to your home that show you *do* care, and that you're creative enough to work with your limited finances and say something unique about yourself."

Indeed, even when makeshift decor is necessary, you can make it work in your favor. My friend Beth has capitalized on her less-than-grand budget by starting a collection of purposely mismatched china. She buys plates one at a time, for pennies, at flea markets and garage sales, and mixes and matches her finds. Beth has created an eclectic look that her dinner guests always admire as creative.

Rather than fighting the inevitability of secondhand goods, Beth celebrates them. Her tiny apartment is filled with flea market finds that she has sanded and refinished herself for an overall look of charm and comfort.

Indeed, flea markets and secondhand shops can be excellent sources for furnishings and for the visual "quirks" that will make your place look more personal and less like a dorm room. My own trips to the local flea market have helped my apartment evolve, in the past two years, from a shrine to prefab to the kind of *home* I can identify with.

When I first moved in, my apartment looked like half a million others across the country. I went out and bought brand-new wall units and a computer cabinet in a go-with-everything oak-veneer finish. The sagging-in-the-middle sofa bed left over from my college apartment was pale gray. Luckily, this was the color of my kitchen cabinets, which you could see from the living room. (They were *in* the living room.)

Despite my instinctive bent for homey furnishings, I went along with the gray and modern basics I had bought or inherited, and outfitted my place in gray and pastel modern. I nailed a gray, black, and pastel poster, in a put-together black plastic frame, on each of the walls. I covered the floor with a pastel dhurrie rug. I made sure that of the 1,024 books I own, only those with gray and pastel jackets were on the coffee table. Next to them was a jar of pastel jelly beans, mixed in with the licorice ones I wouldn't eat on a bet. But they looked so . . . matching. My home was a veritable sea of gray, black, and pastels, with the pieces as perfectly matched in size and color as Farrah Fawcett's teeth.

I thought my apartment looked great, until I realized that it looked nothing like the home of a disorganized, creative, sentimental twenty-three-year-old (me). Rather, it looked like my gynecologist's waiting room. Even the magazines (three-month-old issues, pastel cover photos) were arranged fanlike on the side table—just like in the waiting room. In my determination to replace my mismatched dorm furniture with a cohesively decorated apartment, I had whitewashed any semblance of personality and homeyness.

After six months of chroma-keyed living, I started missing the eclectic personal effects that had made my $275-a-month apartment in Philadelphia so special, and started bringing them from my mother's attic into New York one by one. When my gray sofa bed finally gave out, I replaced it with a bottle-green velvet couch that, while not perfectly matched to my kitchen cabinets, is better suited to my real personality. I took down one of the modern art posters on the foyer wall. Instead, visitors' first view of the apartment included a mélange of small, gilt-framed mirrors and ancient photographs (those of some of my own ancestors, some of whoever sold them at the flea market). One shelf of my modern bookcase was given over to a growing collection of mismatched crystal goblets (Beth's influence, maybe), and another to the not-quite-perfect bowls I made in the ceramics course I took at the "Y" last fall. The apartment was no longer perfectly matched, but it was perfectly me.

To ensure your apartment's perfectly *you,* be sure you're honest with yourself about who you are. Are you a slob? If so, white everything is probably not the best idea, I don't care *how* smashing it looks on the cover of *Metropolitan Home.*

Is your favorite Sunday-afternoon activity a nap on the couch? Don't buy that hard-lined Scandinavian number, then, no matter how classy it looks in the showroom. If you haven't read a book since you finished your oral report on *Catcher in the Rye,* don't waste your money on shelves; a VCR stand might be a better use of your money. To figure out what you need in your apartment, sit down and analyze what you need in your *life.* I asked my survey respondents, "What's the one thing you couldn't live without in your apartment?" Almost everyone listed a TV (though I didn't have one for a year and rarely missed it). Another common answer was a stereo. If you spend a lot of time listening to music, you'll want a good system, so that your tapes don't all sound like old 78s.

Other things listed by recent graduates as absolute necessities included:

Answering machines
The remote control to the TV
My puppy
Pictures of my friends from college
Souvenirs of my postgraduation trip to Spain

"No matter how broke you are, invest in one piece you absolutely love," says my Aunt Ruthe, whose decorating savvy has won her the dubious honor of helping the entire family outfit their homes. "It may be a $10 Superman poster, an antique music stand if you play, a comfortable chair. . . . Whatever it is, it should be something you look forward to coming home to."

Once you've figured out what's going into your apartment, you've got to get it there. Unless you already own massive amounts of furniture, or are moving into a twenty-first-story walk-up, you can probably move your possessions in yourself by station wagon, van, or U-Haul. Enlist the aid of a few close friends, and schlep your possessions yourself, saving *any* mover's charges for the heavy furniture you absolutely can't cart without help.

Furniture you've ordered new can usually be delivered and assembled by the manufacturer or store. And it will probably take a few weeks (or months) to arrive.

While you're waiting for your new furniture to be delivered, you'll have plenty of time to unpack the eighty-four cartons you've lugged along with you, and to get used to your new apartment, its noises, its quirks, and the funny way the left-hand stove burner doesn't light unless you jump on the floor.

Alert your landlord to any repairs that need to be made; they're easier to do before the apartment's cluttered with furniture. Also, if you want to paint, now's the time.

Some landlords will paint before a new tenant moves in if the previous resident left the place a mess. Ask if yours plans to do so, and whether you yourself are allowed to paint. If your landlord allows, you might want to paint the whole apartment, or a small portion of it, in an interest-adding color. Just check if you'll be expected to repaint it white before you leave.

Also, some landlords want you to put enamel, not "flat," paint on the windowsills and trimmings. Check before you buy. Generally, latex paint is your best bet. Pick a color, and calculate how many square feet of wall you have to cover. The paint store salesperson will be able to translate this into gallons for you. While you're there, buy some disposable drop cloths. Pick up a roller, a pan, and a brush, and head home.

If there are cracks in the wall, fill them with ready-mixed spackle compound. If the paint is peeling, scrape off the loose pieces and sandpaper the edges of the cracks. Now you're ready to start painting. First, paint the edges near floor, ceiling, and doors with a brush. Then, roller paint the vast (or not so vast) expanses of wall, rolling as close to the edge as you can. If necessary, roll in one direction first and then go over your work perpendicularly, to get enough color coverage.

Besides painting your walls solid white or magenta, there are lots of other color tricks you can play. My friend Beth (ever the imaginative decorator) has added a touch of color to her bathroom by dipping a sea sponge in blue and green paint and creating a random sponge effect on the walls. (This technique is "technique-ally" called "pouncing.") You can create similar effects with a washcloth, cut-out stencils—use your imagination!

Are you going to carpet the floor? (Many apartment leases stipulate that you must.) If you're planning to lay down a rug that will go under your furniture, put it on the floor before your three-hundred-pound couch is delivered. Wall-to-wall carpeting is not a wise investment unless you're certain you'll be living in one place long enough to get your money's worth. Many carpet stores will bind large square footages of carpet. For example, you can purchase a ten-by-ten-foot expanse of navy blue carpeting and have the edges finished so that it looks like an area rug.

Can you—do you want to—retile your kitchen or bathroom floors? As soon as my friends Cindy and Alison moved into their new apartment, they gave new life to the ugly kitchen. With two hours' worth of work and under $30 worth of peel-and-stick tiles, they said good-bye to the ugly orange linoleum, and hello to a kitchen that doesn't make them lose their appetites. Once in a while, they even use it to make dinner.

23

WHAT Did You Call That Room with the Fridge?

Ah, Yes . . . the Kitchen

Speaking of kitchens, may I point out that if you're paying to have (and retile) one, you might consider using it? A young man of my acquaintance lived in the same apartment for two and a half years and never turned on the oven. Never. He did use the burners once to cook spaghetti, but that was only because the take-out places had closed for Christmas Eve.

Even if you don't know how to boil water, you can learn how to feed yourself. Just ask Stewart Franklin, a friend of mine from high school.

All through college, Stewart lived in a dorm and ate in the cafeteria; his first year in law school, he lived on pizza and ice cream. When, as a 2L, he moved into his own apartment, he decided to learn how to cook.

"I bought a box of macaroni," he told me one night, when

he called in a panic. "And I figured that anything that cost less than a dollar couldn't feed more than one person. So I dumped the whole box into the boiling water." Then his voice rolled to a boiling crescendo. "DO YOU KNOW HOW MUCH MACARONI A WHOLE BOX MAKES?!?!" he shrieked like a man possessed.

Yes, I do. And so would he, if he had read the side of the box. Kitchen rule #1: Read the label. The box tops will give you all sorts of fascinating information, like how much to cook, for how long, and at what temperature. Even Julia Child is rumored to read package directions. Sometimes.

Lots of things come with directions that even a monkey can follow.

"But I can't even scramble an egg," you cry.

So don't. Start out with macaroni, as Stewart did, and work your way up. Pasta comes in enough shapes to keep you busy all year. These days, you can even buy some palatable sauces in the supermarket, though I'll share my recipe with you in case you're feeling adventuresome. To cook and eat pasta, you'll need:

1. A large pot
2. A colander (see below)
3. Salt
4. Water
5. Said pasta
6. Olive oil or butter

Sauces, cheese, and Chianti are optional.

But if you plan on eating more than just linguine, you'll need a slightly better-equipped kitchen. Anyone who has the slightest suspicion he'll be cooking should be sure to own the following essentials:

1. Large (pasta) pot—also good for making soup and using as a mixing bowl.

2. Skillet with 7-inch bottom—for omelets, sautéing things, and making small amounts of pasta.

3. Saucepan—for sauce (hence the name), vegetables (remember them?), and medium-sized amounts of pasta.

4. Nine-by-thirteen-inch baking dish—for Duncan Hines brownies, baked chicken, and, for a change of pace-ta, lasagne.

5. Two or three really good, sharp knives: one all-purpose paring, cutting, chopping knife; a larger knife for cutting raw meats and pineapples; and a serrated (jagged edge) knife for slicing bread and tomatoes.

6. Colander—for draining you-know-what and cooked vegetables; washing fresh veggies.

7. Cutting board.

8. Can opener (you never knew you could eat so much tuna).

9. Pancake turner (for flipping omelets, removing fish from the pan).

10. Vegetable peeler.

11. Plates, silverware, and glasses for the number of people you plan to feed, plus a few extras to guarantee against breakage. (Yes, GUARANTEE: if you buy exactly four place settings, one plate will crack and you'll discover the pattern's irreplaceable. Own a fifth, and your dishes will stay intact, the extra one taking up space you can hardly spare.)

If you're a bit more of a cook, you'll want to expand on this list. But don't buy out the whole housewares department. With a little ingenuity, most kitchen utensils can be used for more than their specific intended purpose, thus saving you room. For example, when you're making pasta for one, you can drain it in a vegetable steamer, or in a sifter—which you'll need if you bake. This will eliminate the need to dig the colander out of the pots-'n'-pans cabinet every time you've boiled up twelve noodles. As I mentioned above, a large stock pot can be used to mix cake batter in, or to store fruit salad in the refrigerator. There's no reason you can't turn your 9-by-13-inch pan over, cover the bottom with tin foil, and use it as a cookie sheet. Or, if you have the cookie sheet but not the bake pan, broil your fish on *that*. Just cover it with tin foil first, or your cookies will smell like smelt.

In time, you can learn to love your kitchen and, who knows, even use it for entertaining. When I'm dining alone, the flip of a coin determines whether I'll sup on pasta or eggs. Sometimes, just for the sheer thrill of it, I break from tradition and open a can of tuna. But when I have company, watch out. "Do you eat like this every night?" my guests often ask. "Not on your life," I often answer. (Other times, I lie.)

Much as I love to cook, my schedule and lack of ambition have rendered me a tuna and take-out type when I'm dining alone. However, I've discovered that making a dinner party for four is cheaper than my one-fourth of a good restaurant meal, so I do it pretty often. If you have three good menus perfected, you can entertain for a year before any of your friends realize that you don't know how to make a fourth dinner. Even when they do, they won't care; most people would rather eat chicken à l'orange at your house for the second time this year than a tuna melt in their own kitchen for the third time this week.

So here are three menus for entertaining that are easily expandable to fit the number of mouths you'll be feeding. These serve four; just multiply or divide.

Easiest Dinner

Tossed Salad
Pasta Putanesca
Garlic Bread
Brownies and Ice Cream

There are two ways to make this dinner: easiest and even more easiest. The latter method is to load up on precut veggies and lettuce at your supermarket's salad bar, decant bottled dressing into a cruet. Cover the pasta with a jar of standard spaghetti sauce to which you've added a quarter cup of red wine and a few extra minced garlic cloves while the sauce is simmering. Duncan Hines brownies are designed for a first-grader's use, and Häagen-Dazs is ubiquitous. If you're too lazy to make garlic bread, even that can be bought in the supermarket. Just heat it up so that it's warm and crispy.

If you'd like to feel a little more . . . well, involved, in this dinner party, you can make the salad dressing, sauce, and brownies from scratch. All can be made a few days in advance and refrigerated (freeze the brownies) and heated up right before chow time.

Mustard Vinaigrette

Ingredients

- **½ cup extra-virgin olive oil**
- **½ cup red wine vinegar**
- **Pinch sugar**
- **1 teaspoon Dijon mustard**
- **1 teaspoon dried tarragon, crumbled**

How To

Whisk all ingredients together with a fork. Shake or stir again right before serving.

Putanesca Sauce

Ingredients

2 small onions
5 cloves garlic
1/4 cup olive oil
10 medium-sized fresh mushrooms
1 green pepper
1 6-ounce can tomato paste
12 ounces red wine
1 teaspoon dried thyme
1 tablespoon basil
1 tablespoon oregano
1/2 teaspoon salt
1 teaspoon black pepper
1 28-ounce can crushed tomatoes
1 tablespoon capers
10 black olives
3 anchovies
3 dashes Tabasco

How To

Mince the onions and garlic, and sauté in the olive oil in a large pot. Do not allow them to brown. Chop the mushrooms and add them to the pot. Dice the pepper and add it, as well. Add the tomato paste. Fill the now-empty can twice with red wine, and add that, too. Add the herbs, salt, and pepper and simmer for 15 minutes. Add the crushed tomatoes and the rest of the ingredients and let the whole thing boil away. Reduce heat to a simmer (leaving the cover off the pot) and let the sauce cook until you're ready to serve it. It should simmer for at least 1 hour; the longer the better. If sauce gets too thick, add a drop more wine or some water.

The sauce will keep in the refrigerator for about 5 days, or it can be frozen.

Kahlúa Brownies

Ingredients

1 6-ounce bag semisweet chocolate chips
4 eggs
1 1/4 cups sugar
10 tablespoons butter (1 stick plus 2 tablespoons; the measurements are marked on the side of the wrapper)
1 tablespoon Kahlúa or Tia Maria coffee liqueur
1 tablespoon strong instant coffee (not granules; mix the granules with hot water and then measure 1 tablespoon)
1 cup flour
1 teaspoon baking powder (from the can; baking soda comes in a box)
1/4 teaspoon salt

How To

Melt the chocolate by putting it in a Pyrex measuring cup or other heatproof container immersed in a few inches of water simmering in a pan (or use a double boiler, which is the right way to do things, if you're fussy). In a bowl, beat eggs, sugar, and butter until the mixture is light and fluffy. Add the liqueur and the coffee, and stir. Now add this goop to the melted chocolate and stir well.

Sift the dry ingredients right into this bowl, and mix everything together. Bake at 350 degrees in a greased 9-by-13 baking pan for half an hour, or until a fork inserted into the middle comes out without batter stuck to it.

The next meal is slightly more expensive to prepare, and it's more impressive, but it's still pretty easy.

Crudités and Dips
Chicken and Apples in Puff Pastry
Glazed Carrots
Green Beans Amandine
Sorbet and Chocolates

Crudités and Dips

Cut up fresh vegetables: carrots, broccoli florets, string beans—use whatever's pretty and available. Arrange these in groups, by vegetable, in a small wicker basket or on a plate. Serve with a selection of the following dips:

1. Equal parts of sour cream, Dijon mustard, and honey
2. A jar of roasted red peppers you've drained well and puréed in the blender or food processor, to which you've added a sprinkle of hot red pepper or a dash of Tabasco
3. Russian or bleu cheese dressing from a jar

Experiment: Add different crazy things (try chutney or jarred pesto) to mayonnaise, sour cream, or plain yogurt, and see what happens.

Chicken and Apples in Puff Pastry

Ingredients

4 half chicken breasts, skinned and boned (you can buy them this way)
1 1-pound box frozen puff pastry
Apricot or red currant jam
1 apple, peeled and cored

How To

Rinse the chicken breasts and pat dry. Roll out the pastry to ¼-inch thickness, and cut four squares, each of which is large enough to envelop one chicken cutlet. Spread each square of pastry lightly with jam.

Slice the apple thinly, and put slices on each chicken breast. Place a chicken breast with apple on each square of pastry (don't worry if it doesn't look beautiful; it will when you're finished). Wrap the pastry around chicken and apples, and pinch shut.

Bake the bundles on a lightly oiled baking tin at 400 degrees for 30 to 45 minutes, until pastry is golden brown.

Glazed Carrots

Ingredients

1 1-pound bag of fresh carrots
½ cup frozen orange juice concentrate
1 tablespoon butter or margarine
1 teaspoon dried ground ginger

How To

Scrape and clean the carrots. Cut into round slices. In a medium-sized saucepan, boil carrots in water till semi-tender, about 20 minutes. Drain carrots and return to pan with other ingredients. Cook on low heat until carrots are cooked through, about another 15 minutes.

Green Beans Amandine

Ingredients

1 bag frozen French-style green beans
2 tablespoons butter
1 cup slivered almonds

How To

Defrost green beans. Heat over low flame until cooked but still bright green (about 5 minutes). In skillet, melt butter and toast nuts for about 10 minutes. Pour nuts and butter over beans and serve.

Sorbet and Chocolates

How To

Buy them at the store. Pick an unusual flavor (mango? boysenberry?) and the finest chocolates you can afford. Minimalist extravagance.

Finally, here's a menu to pull out when you're trying to impress:

Salmon Pâté and Pumpernickel
New Potatoes with Crème Fraîche and Caviar
Asparagus Salad
Fish in Mustard-Vermouth Sauce
Zucchini in Light Garlic Butter
Rice Pilaf
Chocolate Mousse

Salmon Pâté

Ingredients

1 7½-ounce can red salmon
1 3-ounce package cream cheese (not whipped)
1 small onion
1 bunch fresh dill
½ cup unflavored dry bread crumbs
1 teaspoon black pepper

How To

Mix all ingredients well in a blender or food processor and spoon into a bowl or crock. Refrigerate 3 hours or overnight. Serve with slices of pumpernickel bread.

New Potatoes with Crème Fraîche and Caviar

Ingredients

8 small new (red) potatoes
Vegetable oil
½ cup crème fraîche (get it at a gourmet store) or sour cream
1 jar salmon, whitefish, or lumpfish roe

How To

Boil potatoes till just tender (about 20 minutes). Coat lightly with vegetable oil and refrigerate till cold. Cut each potato in two, the long way (you should have two oval halves left). With a teaspoon, remove a spoonful of potato pulp from each half. Replace this with a dollop of cream and a spoonful of the caviar.

Asparagus Salad

Ingredients

1 bunch thin asparagus, cleaned and trimmed
1 small jar roasted sweet red peppers
1 tablespoon sesame oil
4 slices of lemon

How To

Cook asparagus in boiling water till barely tender, about 7 minutes. Remove from pot, immerse in ice-cold water, and put in refrigerator to chill. Drain peppers and chop them coarsely. Mix peppers with sesame oil. Arrange asparagus on each plate, with spears all pointing in the same direction. Pour pepper mixture over the bottom third of each bunch. Garnish each plate with a slice of lemon.

Fish in Mustard-Vermouth Sauce

Ingredients

4 medium-sized fresh fish steaks (halibut, salmon trout, swordfish)
2 cups dry vermouth
½ cup honey mustard (or ¼ cup each Dijon mustard and honey)
2 tablespoons dried tarragon

How To

Place fish steaks in a 10-inch nonstick skillet and cover with vermouth. Simmer for 10 minutes, then flip steaks over and simmer 5 more minutes. Add honey mustard and tarragon and stir, being careful not to chop up fish. Raise heat to high and keep stirring, cooking another 5 minutes or until fish is opaque all the way through. As the fish cooks, the liquid evaporates, leaving a delicious sauce with the consistency of chocolate syrup.

Zucchini in Light Garlic Butter

Ingredients

2 cloves garlic, minced
Olive oil
2 zucchini

How To

Sauté minced garlic in oil for about 5 minutes. Dice zucchini. Add zucchini to garlic and oil and sauté for additional 15 minutes over low heat.

Rice Pilaf

Ingredients

2½ cups chicken or vegetable broth (instant is fine)
1 tablespoon butter
½ cup rice
¼ cup chopped pecans
¼ cup chopped fresh parsley

How To

Bring broth to a boil. Add butter and rice and cook, covered, for 20 minutes. Let rice stand for about 5 minutes, then add nuts and parsley.

Chocolate Mousse

Ingredients

6 ounces semisweet chocolate chips
3 eggs
1 teaspoon vanilla or amaretto
Dash of salt
¼ cup heavy cream, whipped

How To

Melt chocolate in a double boiler, over hot water. Separate eggs, placing whites in a small bowl. Beat yolks slightly with a fork. Add vanilla or amaretto, and salt. Blend into chocolate. Beat egg whites until soft peaks form. Beat in sugar. Slowly fold in chocolate, only until well blended. Then, gently fold in whipped cream. Chill until serving time.

If you want to expand your repertoire beyond these three menus, you can get a few good cookbooks and start practicing. The James Beard series gives pretty clear directions, as do the books by Craig Claiborne and Pierre Franey. This duo has also put together a series of cookbooks for meals in under an hour.

If you're unsure about which dishes go with what others, the *New York Times* has published a menu cookbook, as has James Beard. *Julia Child and Company* is also a good source for menu and recipe plans, but her dinners tend to be a bit more complicated than the others I've listed here.

If your passion for cooking and entertaining really takes off, you can start experimenting with ethnic specialties, teaching yourself from books or at courses given at local continuing-ed centers.

But remember that when guests come, they're coming (we hope) more for a good time than for a good meal. If you're shaky about your cooking skills, stick to basics. Just keep the wine and conversation flowing, and no one will notice or care that dinner consists of dressed-up take-out.

And take-out can be dressed up. If you often serve delivered Chinese food, invest in some pretty carved chopsticks (they can range from 50 cents to $10 a pair). If you're keeping the sushi house in business, see if you can find lacquer stands to serve the fish on. Remove everything from the cartons out of guests' sight, and serve on a pretty tablecloth and napkins. Your guests will know you're making an effort on their behalf, and that's what really matters.

When you've filled your apartment, no matter how small it is, with things and people you love, it will start to feel like a home—that special place you look forward to returning to after a long day at work or a long night of bar hopping. There really is no place like it.

24

Breakfast, Lunch, and Dinner of Champions

What You Need to Know About Nutrition

The menus in the preceding chapter are relatively healthful. Relatively. Eat like that for a year, and they'll use you as the backup airship in the Goodyear fleet of blimps. Now that you're sitting on your backside all day, it's going to be a little tougher to keep it small enough to fit on the chair. Even if you're dying to *gain* weight (I hate you. I really hate you), you need to start thinking about healthful eating; your twenties is when the arteries start to clog.

In terms of long-term health, the two most basic—and most important—nutritional commandments are:

- Eat more fiber.
- Eat less fat.

This will benefit your heart, stomach, and skin, as well as your health. According to the American Cancer Society, a diet that's low in fats and high in fiber can reduce your risk of several forms of cancer. The ACS also recommends that, to minimize your risk of disease, you include dark green and deep yellow fruits and vegetables rich in vitamins A and C. Also include cabbage, broccoli, Brussels sprouts, kohlrabi, and cauliflower. Be moderate in consumption of salt-cured, smoked, and nitrite-cured foods (e.g., bacon, frankfurters). And, again, eat fiber and avoid fats.

But wait. Before you try to ingest more fiber by biting into a bran muffin, know that many of the commercial variety are as overstuffed as your grandmother's sofa, full of fats and sodium. The largest bakery muffins can pack as much as seven hundred calories—close to half of what a relatively sedentary young adult should be eating daily.

Nutritionist Gail Levey, M.S., R.D., offers the following bran muffin recipe as a substitute for the cakelike ones that sabotage your diet.

Dry Ingredients

3 cups wheat bran (not bran cereal)
1¼ cups white flour
½ cup sugar
1½ teaspoons baking soda
1 teaspoon cinnamon

Wet Ingredients

2 cups lowfat buttermilk
1 egg
¼ cup safflower or corn oil

Fruits and Nuts

Choice A: **¾ cup each white and dark raisins, and ½ cup chopped walnuts**

or

Choice B: **1 cup chopped dried apricots, ½ cup chopped walnuts**

How To

Mix dry ingredients together. Beat wet ingredients together very well and add to dry mix. You can put them all in a jar and shake, or use an eggbeater or blender. Fold in fruits and nuts. Bake in lightly oiled muffin tins at 425 degrees for about 20 minutes, or until a knife inserted into the center of a muffin comes out clean. Let cool before removing from pan. Muffins can be frozen and toasted daily for breakfast.

In general, you need to be eating food that, like Levey's muffins, gives you as many nutrients per bite as possible.

If you don't have the time to bake them—or the mathematical skills to compute how many grams of fat are in their store-bought counterpart—pick up a copy of *The Living Heart—Brand Name Shopper's Guide* by DeBakey, Gotto, Scott, and Foreyt (Master Media). It will tell you which items on your grocer's shelf fall within the now-accepted-as-gospel guidelines of less than 30 percent calories from fat and which are low in cholesterol. Remember that not every product with a "low fat" or "lite" banner is really good for you. Some are high in sodium; others have absolutely no nutritional value. So instead of looking at the puffery, look at the package information. It will tell you whether it's worth popping that product into your shopping cart—and your system.

"As you get older, and as you move from a life in which you ran around to one in which you sit behind a desk, you have to get more bang for your nutritional buck," says Bonnie Liebman, M.S., director of nutrition at the Center for Science in the Public Interest in Washington, D.C. "You have to pack as many nutrients as possible into the food choices you make."

Before you resign yourself to a life of tofu and raw buckwheat, realize that healthy food doesn't have to be 1970s-style "health food."

"The trick to eating wisely," says Liebman, "is to have the right stuff around." If you have cookies and candy readily accessible in your apartment, with vegetables no nearer than the grocer three towns over, it's not hard to guess who'll be having Snickers à la mode for dinner. A lot of the "right stuff," Liebman notes, isn't any harder to prepare than junk food.

"People think the easiest thing is to pop in a TV dinner," she says. "In fact, you can broil a piece of fish in just as little time, and if you have a microwave, a baked potato can be ready in minutes." Even if you're baking your spud in a traditional oven, it requires no attention. You can pop it in and talk on the phone, do your sit-ups, or watch the news while it cooks.

"Another idea," says Liebman, "is to bake a chicken at the beginning of the week. You can slice it for sandwiches all week long."

If you like chicken salad as much as I do, but are as wary of mayonnaise, try my favorite dietetic chicken salad:

Cut up some cold, cooked chicken. Dump in some defrosted frozen string beans (the round ones, not "French-style"). Add halved cherry tomatoes and black olives. Coat lightly with Dijon mustard, and sprinkle on some tarragon.

Bonnie Liebman also recommends pasta (which is probably why I hit it off with her so well in our interview). Just stay away from buttery or cheese-laden sauces, she cautions, as these can pump lots of artery-clogging cholesterol into your system. One of her favorite quick sauces is a sauté of canned clams, onions, and mushrooms in olive oil.

Another fast and healthy way to prepare pasta is by dumping on top of it some diced tomato, a can of tuna, some olives, and some marinated artichoke hearts. Any of these meals is even healthier if you start or finish with fresh vegetables or fruits. If you can't use up a head of lettuce before it spoils, cut up cucumber and carrot sticks, or munch on zucchini rounds.

If you work crazy hours, dinner won't always be a 6:00 P.M. affair. You may eat lunch on the run and skip breakfast altogether. But there's good news, says Liebman: "It's not as important when you eat as what you eat." The claim that breakfast is the most important meal of the day has never been substantiated, except in research studies sponsored by cereal companies. "Some people simply aren't hungry until noon. They shouldn't force themselves to eat beforehand." The one thing to be wary of, though, is skipping breakfast because you're trying to lose weight, or because you think you won't be hungry till lunch, and then capitulating to a croissant craving at 10:00 A.M.

The office coffee cart can be deadly, especially if you have to watch your weight, and the vending machines are no better. "If you're going to be working late, bring some fruit to work," Liebman says. Again and again, the theme of planning ahead comes through. If you keep healthy food at your fingertips, you're less likely to stick them into a bag of nacho chips.

All of this sounds commonsensible, when you think about it. Most of us, though, barely have enough time to eat, let alone time to think about it. As a result, most of those who answered my survey admitted to having horrible eating habits. Some nutritional regimens included:

"Chocolate, soda, and more chocolate."

"Nothing that can't be delivered in fifteen minutes or less."

"Junk, junk, and more junk. I eat junky lunches and I

never have time for dinner, so I just eat more junk before I go to bed."

"More Chinese food than Mao Tse-tung could digest."

A few respondents, though, described eating habits even a grandmother would approve of:

"Lots of everything, but nothing in excess."

"Three square meals and a piece of fruit before bed."

"I eat a lot of salad, and some chicken and fish."

Interestingly enough, there was a positive correlation between the respondents' reported stress levels and the amount of junk food in their respective diets: The busier and more stressed-out my subjects claimed to be, the worse their eating habits. This just re-proves Bonnie Liebman's point: the busier you are, the more important it is to make sure that when you're just "reaching for whatever's in the refrigerator," whatever's in the refrigerator is good for you.

Some good news: according to Gail Levey, no one's ever proven the myth that bodies under stress need different or more nutrients. "The amount of vitamin C you lose by running around all day can be made up with a few slices of orange," she says. "Really, there's no difference between how a high-power person should eat and how someone who sits in front of the TV all day should eat, assuming they're burning the same amount of calories."

If you are a high-power person, or are striving to become one, your body may not need gallons of extra OJ . . . but it will need good care and attention—yours and that of a doctor.

25

Is There a Doctor in the House?

Finding Quality Medical Care

Your hands are shaking, your fever's rising, and your stomach feels as if it were just attacked by terrorists. If you're not dressing for a date, these are probably signs that you're sick.

"I'll just walk down to Student Health," you think—only to remember that the free campus clinic, where you used to pick up medical help and freshmen, is now five hundred miles away.

So, just when you're so bleary-eyed you can barely find your toes, you have to find a doctor. If you're living close to where you grew up, chances are you already know a good physician in town. However, if you're still using the pediatrician who gave you your first monthly checkup twenty-two years ago, it's time to find a new medicine man. Otherwise, you'll soon notice that you're older than some of the parents waiting with this year's crop of colicky infants.

If your parents are nearby, you can use their internist or general practitioner. By "nearby," I mean close enough for you to make the trek home not only when you're healthy and in search of a free meal, but also when you're sick enough to need a doctor. If your family physician is too far away for you realistically to go home for an appointment, look for a more local physician.

Alan D'Alessio, a Miami real estate broker, lives "close enough" to his Ft. Lauderdale parents and their physician that he hasn't bothered finding a new doctor in Miami. Yet, when he's sick enough to warrant a visit to the doctor, the last thing in the world he wants to do is drive forty-five minutes up the highway.

"I never go to the doctor except for my checkup," Alan says ironically. "I hate trekking up there when I'm sick. I guess I probably should find a doctor close by," he says. Yes, he probably should. And so should you.

In fact, the "official" recommendation is to find a doctor as soon as you move into town (when you're healthy) and go for a baseline checkup. That way, when the doctor sees you as a sick patient, he or she can make comparisons to your healthy state. The American Medical Association recommends that people have checkups around age twenty-one, and at least every five years thereafter until age forty, when annual checkups become crucial.

If you're trying to establish a rapport with your doctor that could prove crucial if and when you do get sick, you'll want to go for checkups more frequently.

Despite the sense in finding a doctor and having regular checkups, many of us work on the "if it ain't broke, don't fix it" schedule, and visit doctors only when we're sick. In fact, most of us wait until we're sick as puppies to find a new doctor. I had always assumed that when I returned to New York, I would continue to use the physician who had treated me since junior high school. But like Alan D'Alessio, I found that while I didn't mind a two-hour odyssey that included trains, buses, and taxis when I needed a checkup (okay, I minded a little), I *certainly* wasn't going to embark on the incredible journey when I was miserably sick.

During my first year on the job, I had what I described as "that horrible cheap-Mexican-food feeling" for a week. Because my doctor was so inconveniently located, I resisted calling him; the only thing worse than the feeling in the pit of my stomach was the dread that filled that bodily region as I contemplated the journey to the suburbs.

After ten days of internal warfare, I was finally convinced that this was a case in which gastric relief would have to be spelled d-o-c-t-o-r, and fast. My boss gave me her husband-the-physician's phone number, and he's been curing my ails—and those of several of my friends—ever since.

If you've foolishly gone to work for someone who's married to an attorney, museum curator, or truck driver, you'll need to find your physician some other way.

One good way to find a doctor is to ask friends who've grown up in town—or who've lived there for a few years—for recommendations. Or ask the doctor you used back home. One caveat in the latter case: your pediatrician's med school buddy may have been a terrific study partner forty years ago. This doesn't guarantee he hasn't turned into an incompetent practitioner. Make sure the doctor who's doing the recommending has seen the object of his approval "in action" lately.

If you are having trouble finding a new doctor through

word of mouth, or finding someone whose recommendation you trust, call the best-reputed hospital in town. Many hospitals have physician-referral services that will put you in touch with the specialist (or generalist) who's good for what ails you. Mike Brooks, who moved to Santa Fe after graduation to work in hotel management, found his doctor through a local hospital. "They gave me three names. I just picked one of the three out of a hat, and I was satisfied with him. If I hadn't been, I could have called either of the other two, or asked the hospital for more names." This system seems to be pretty standard. I checked out a couple of hospitals across the country and found that, indeed, they work on a random rotating basis. At Massachusetts General Hospital, for example, the internal medicine department has one service, while subspecialties such as surgery and orthopedics share another. When a prospective patient calls, the service gives the names of three physicians for him to call. From there, it's up to him to call the physician and arrange for a consultation. The physicians' names are given out on a rotating basis; presumably, then, you have as much chance of getting the best doctor in the department as the worst. That's why it's important to be a savvy consumer. I'll go into more details on this later; for now, let me strongly urge you to follow up the referral program's referral with your own thorough assessment of the doctor's suitability.

If your company has a staff physician, or a doctor who's connected with the firm, check out that option. Bill Edmund has been using the wellness center at his company headquarters since he began work two years ago. "It's right here, and I don't have to deal with any finances or insurance hassles," he says. "The doctors are pretty good—most of them are private practice doctors who staff our clinic.

Why should I pay their office rates when I can get the same good care right at work?"

If there is a doctor at your office, check out how this fits into your insurance plan. If the company doctor is the only one covered by your plan, he or she should (assuming competence and comfort) be your first choice.

Another increasingly popular option is the HMO—or health maintenance organization—a setup that is, again, often linked to your health care benefits package. Talk to your company benefits administrator if you're not sure what your options are under the company coverage.

If you're self-employed or working for someone who does not offer medical insurance, cover your own ass (and ulcer; and broken arm). See if you can still be covered under your parents' plan. (Many plans allow for inclusion of children up to the age of twenty-three. If there is an extra charge to your folks, it might still be cheaper for you to reimburse them than to get your own plan.) But even if you do have to get your own plan, do so. The monthly premiums for young, healthy people are not that high. The worst thing that can happen (actually, the *best* thing that can happen) is you pay in but never get sick enough to cash in. Lucky you. But what would you do if you had no insurance and had to be hospitalized for six months? Think about it. And while you're thinking about it, call a few insurance agencies and ask for information.

No matter how you pay for your doctor's visits, remember that your first trek to the office is like a visit to one of those vacation villages that invite you through the mail: there is NO OBLIGATION. If you don't like a doctor, don't use him. (You will, obviously, have to pay for your office visit regardless of whether you plan to return to the doctor.)

Remember at all times that *you* are the consumer here. Just as your doctor will have a list of questions for you, you should be completing a mental checklist as you determine whether this particular physician suits your needs.

In evaluating a doctor, take a look at the office walls—but don't be guided by the academic wallpaper alone. Diplomas are important, but they're not the bottom line; *someone* has to graduate at the bottom of the class at Harvard Med School. You're better off with a "star" from a good state medical college than with an Ivy League imbecile.

Start by inquiring where your doctor did his training. Is she board-certified in a specialty? Where does he have admitting privileges? In other words, if you require hospitalization, will you be in a topflight institution or in a fly-by-night butchery where you'd rather not go even for a pedicure?

How old is the doctor? If you're looking to establish a long-term relationship with a physician so that he or she can see you through the end of Oxy 10 and the beginning of Geritol, you probably shouldn't start seeing a doctor who's six months away from retirement. On the other hand, someone who's still waving the med school diploma to dry the ink probably isn't your best bet either. Try to find a doctor whose formal training is still relevant to medicine as it's practiced in the 1990s, but who also has the real-life experience to back up those eighty-three years med students all spend in the lab. In short, you're best advised to look for someone halfway between doctors Marcus Welby and Doogie Howser.

Selecting a physician is one area in which it is perfectly acceptable (advisable, even) to be a snob. Don't hesitate to inquire how the doctor has been recognized for excellence.

Is she a fellow in the American Academy of her specialty? Does he hold other academic or teaching honors? Is he widely quoted in the press? Beware: This isn't *always* a guarantee of excellence. If you see a doctor quoted in the press or interviewed on TV, it means one of two things:

1. He is truly an expert in the field.
2. He has made a career out of spokespersonship, and cares more about the guy on the other side of the camera than the one on the other side of the stethoscope.

When I worked in health care public relations, I spent six months booking a media tour for a rheumatologist. His own hands were crippled from being so tightly curled around the wads of bills he earned for his TV appearances. As a result, I'm wary of any physician whose first name is "And our next guest is . . ."

A famous doctor does you no good if you can't get an appointment until after his six-month media tour, or if you only get to see his right-out-of-school associate. Since you never know when you're going to get sick, you'll want a physician who is accessible when you need her. While *no one* makes house calls anymore, phone calls are still in vogue. There's no reason for your doctor not to return yours. Be sure to find out who returns her calls and takes care of her patients while she's away.

You also have to be comfortable with your physician as a person: does he or she take enough time to answer your questions, without making you feel stupid for asking them? You have the right to ask your doctor *any* question about your body, your illness, and its treatment, and to ask again if the first answer is given in medical jargon. No doctor will know all the answers immediately; don't trust anyone who pretends to.

It's important that your doctor's philosophies about

medical/ethical issues are similar to your own. If you get pregnant and wish to have an abortion, will your physician perform one? If you're a right-to-lifer, can you be sure your doctor won't try to talk you into something you're opposed to? If you become terminally ill, will the doctor you've chosen abide by your wishes to sustain life (or not) through artificial means? Ideally, your physician should be someone who has the medical knowledge to care for your body the way *you* think it should be cared for. If you've been seeing a chiropractor for ten years of successful back-pain management, and your new doctor thinks chiropractors are charlatans, you may have a mismatch here. Again, be sure you're comfortable with your doctor's answers to your "interview" questions. Don't be less fussy choosing a doctor than you are when picking a hairdresser.

Even when you've found a doctor you're pleased with, keep asking questions. "What are the potential side effects of this medication?" "How long should I expect my recovery to take?" "Should I restrict my physical activity or change my diet?" Taking charge of your own health will help you safeguard it; for maximum health, keep actively seeking and offering information.

Now let's look at the flip side of this Curious George routine. You have to feel comfortable answering questions as well as asking them. You may not want to tell your doctor everything about your personal life, but you should feel comfortable doing so if necessary. Some medical conditions will require you to share with your doctor the details of your eating, drug, and sexual habits. Within the bounds of normal shyness, you should feel comfortable providing honest answers.

Once you and your doctor have exchanged information in the course of his taking your medical history (which should also include questions about your parents' and siblings' health and any conditions that run in the family), the actual physical examination takes place. It should include a stem-to-stern check of all your vital organs with inspections of all limbs and orifices, as well as a blood pressure check. A complete blood work-up should include a blood count, renal function, tests of your liver, cholesterol, and blood glucose, and other chemical checks of your health state.

All of these questions, checks, and tests will take at least an hour. Consider it an investment in your long-term health care.

The foregoing consumer-protective guidelines apply not only to your general doctor, but also to any specialists you need. If you have a chronic knee problem, for example, you should find a local orthopedist. The bespectacled among you will need an ophthalmologist (have your prescription checked every two years), and women will need a gynecologist with whom to schedule yearly visits.

According to the American College of Obstetricians and Gynecologists, women over eighteen should have three consecutive, annual negative Pap smears and then see their gynecologist every two years. If any of your tests is at all suspect, you should continue to visit annually or as often as your doctor recommends. Furthermore, if you or your partner is not monogamous, you should be examined every year. Some sexually transmitted diseases (STDs), like chlamydia, have no symptoms, but can lead to long-term fertility problems. A quick and painless test performed as part of a routine exam can screen for this and other diseases.

While we're on the subject of STDs, three quick words of advice: condom, condom, condom. It is estimated that one in every eight college-aged adults contracts a sexually transmitted disease. This includes honors students, rising young attorneys, and the sweetest girl you ever met. Sexually transmitted diseases don't discriminate. Therefore, *you* have to. Be selective about whom you sleep with, and take every precaution you can to shield yourself from disease. These days, it's not overly dramatic to say that the life you save may, indeed, be your own.

26

The Doctor Will/Won't See You Now

Knowing When to Call the Doctor and When to Skip Work

Once you've found a doctor, how do you know when to call? The first determination to make is whether what you need is medical attention—or sympathy. If all you need is someone to promise you that your hangover is not fatal, call your college roommate. If your tummy hurts because you still haven't quite gotten the spaghetti sauce recipe down pat (ah! that minor difference between a "clove" and a "head" of garlic!!), call Doctor Mom.

If your illness is more organic in nature, though, it may be time to call in the hired guns (and needles). According to Kirk Zachary M.D., a gastroenterologist/internist in Manhattan, you should call your doctor immediately if you experience any of the following symptoms: severe abdominal pain accompanied by vomiting or nausea; high fever; blood in your urine or stool; suspicion that you have a sexually transmitted disease; or chest pains (yes, even at our age). Most flus, colds, or viruses should resolve themselves in three to five days. If you're sick for longer than that, or have a persistent cough, Dr. Zachary advises that you call the doctor.

Hairshirts went out in the Middle Ages; if you're sick enough to need a doctor, don't be too proud to call one. When retail sales trainee Kevin Kennedy got the flu last year, he braved the Chicago winter to go to the store through two weeks of illness. "If I were still at school, I definitely would have cut class when I was sick like that," the twenty-four-year-old says. "I'm sufficiently motivated by work, though, that I felt I had to go. It was the middle of the Christmas shopping season."

While Kevin's dedication is commendable, a work-till-you-drop philosophy isn't always beneficial. First of all, if you're contagious, you run the risk of infecting your whole department. Furthermore, rest is the best cure for many illnesses. It's likely that if Kevin had stayed home for two days, he would have been better—and twice as productive—after one week, rather than two.

Rest may, in fact, be the best cure for the symptom that sends many young adults to their doctors: fatigue. Recently, these ache-y, worn-out feelings have been identified as a syndrome called chronic Epstein-Barr virus. This disease, which shares many identifying symptoms with the mono you suffered from freshman year, can linger for years. In fact, several support groups have sprung up across the country to aid CEBV sufferers deal with the fact that they're not going to get better. If you are diagnosed, your physician or the local hospital can recommend one of these groups if you think it would be helpful.

Epstein-Barr virus strikes mostly young professionals in

urban areas, and as such has been nicknamed the "yuppie flu." Simply being a tired yuppie, though, doesn't mean you've got CEBV; like sun-dried tomatoes, the virus has become overly chic. As a result, the ubiquitous ailment gets blamed for a lot more snoring than it's responsible for. Many tired people (or their doctors) who assume CEBV are really dealing with another malady, with an easier to remember name: overwork. In other words, if you need a Sunday-afternoon nap or an extra can of Coke to make it through the day, don't assume you have this pinstriped ailment. You may just be *tired*. Use common sense in calling your doctor, says Dr. Zachary. If you go for a checkup every time you're feeling run-down, you can end up spending a lot of money on unnecessary medical care. Conversely, if you *are* really tired for a really long time, you should let the doctor know. You may be suffering from anemia, hepatitis, mono, or, really, from Epstein-Barr.

Whatever the diagnosis of your condition, if you are going to miss work due to illness, be sure to call in first thing in the morning. Your boss doesn't need a sneeze-by-sneeze description of your ailment. . . . Just say, "I have a virus [or the flu, or a fractured hip] and I'll be back in the office as soon as I possibly can." Gory details are neither necessary nor appreciated. A tally of how many times you ran to the bathroom last night is of interest to no one but your mother.

If the doctor has ordered you to stay in bed for a certain period of time, let your boss know up front that you'll be out for a week, or three days, or whatever. Leave your home number in case there's an absolute emergency and your boss needs to know how you labeled the Cincinnati project file on your computer disk.

When you're well enough to be back at work, but still

sick enough to complain, resist the temptation to do so. Alerting others to your allergies, backache, or migraine will only make them nervous that you'll give them your germs, your sob story, and your work.

If you walk around the office complaining about headaches, backaches, and ulcers, your supervisors are likely to think you're unfit for the tasks at hand. Better to try to resolve your stress-causing situations without using your illness for excuse or leverage. If you're truly being overworked, sit down with your boss to discuss ways in which you can restructure your days to keep everyone's lives simpler. This will mark you as an eager beaver, rather than a lame duck.

27

Passing the Stress Test

How to Keep Daily Pressures from Getting You Down

If your work really *is* making you sick, you're in good, if miserable, company.

In the questionnaires I handed out, every respondent except one agreed that work is more stressful than school. On a scale of 1 to 10, with 10 being the highest, the average grade my subjects gave to work stress was an overwhelming 8.5.

It is estimated that 35 percent of all medical ailments have their basis in stress. In addition, Carol Wilkinson, M.D., a doctor in New York City who has had a corporate practice, believes that stress is probably a contributing factor in 70 percent of all physical ills.

"With job uncertainty and constant effort to best increasing competition as two of the few constants in our business world, it is not surprising that the work environment has become unpredictable and frenetic," write Robert and Madeleine Swain in *Out the Organization* (MasterMedia).

The day-to-day stresses of living in a big city can take their toll, too, says psychologist Alice Juskowitz. As the number of homeless on the streets rises, for example, many of us are walking around with feelings of sadness, helplessness, or anger at the more aggressive beggars who harass us daily. "Most people can reduce this stress," says Dr. Juskowitz, "if they take meaningful action. Volunteer in a soup kitchen or write letters of protest to your elected officials. This isn't going to solve the problem, but it will help you feel as if you are doing something to make your city a less dangerous place. The same is true for environmental problems: organize a boycott, circulate a petition. Besides being empowering, these actions can be *fun,* if you do them in a large group."

When you can't avoid stress, try sweating it out. Literally. Studies show that vigorous exercise causes the brain to release chemicals that act as natural mood calmers. These endorphins, as they are called, act as natural tranquilizers, and can help restore emotional equilibrium. (Or, after a workout, you may be too worn out to be stressed out; the vote's not yet in.)

On a more basic level, if you pretend that tennis ball you're attacking is your boss's head, or that the kicks you're doing in aerobics class are really landing in your roommate's gut, you may just feel better when you're finished. Many runners insist that they feel better after a few laps around the park. Personally, I prefer a l-o-n-g walk. Both my mood and the shape of my calves are the better for it.

If you're not a pavement pounder, there are countless

other workout options available to you. If your apartment complex has a pool and/or gym, you can work out there. In addition to the convenience, these setups offer social benefits as well. In many places, the bench press has replaced the park bench as ideal neighbor-meeting place. If there's no gym *in* your home, find one near enough either to your residence or to your office so that it's really convenient. If you have to trek three miles just to get to the locker room, you're less likely to get the most out of your health club membership.

When selecting a health club, try to find one that fits not only into your commuting schedule but into your workout timetable as well. Check the club out during the time of day you'll actually be using it. If everyone else who belongs to your gym shares your need to work out between 5:30 and 7:00 P.M., you may find you spend more time cooling your heels than stretching your hamstrings. At peak hours, the waits for the weight machines can be up to fifteen minutes each, turning what should be a twenty-minute Nautilus circuit into an all-night affair.

If you can't find a suitable place to work out indoors (and even if you can), look outside. Rather than spending $500 to wait twenty minutes each night for your turn at a stationary bike, you may want to spend that same money on the moving variety. Bike riding is a great way to tone your thighs and condition your heart as well as a wonderful means of exploring your city and the countryside that lies beyond it. Even if you *do* belong to a gym, you may want to hold on to your old bike for summer picnics and rides through the neighborhood.

Many of the learning extension centers that are springing up across the country quicker than crabgrass (e.g., Learning Annex, Discovery Center) offer bike trips that can help you slim your thighs while you fatten your "little black book." They're really a great way to meet people. My friend Lisa has a whole new crop of friends to go jazz-club hopping with since she took a two-session jazz class.

Some of these schools-without-walls also offer more off-beat fitness/socializing options, including horseback riding, tango dancing, and fencing. Find one that strikes your fancy and give it a try. You may open up a whole new hobby and way of meeting people.

Team sports are another great way to combine physical and social pursuits. If your company has a softball or volleyball team, join. If you're as lazy or inhibited as I am, at least be a cheerleader. After watching *About Last Night* several more times than that B movie warranted, my hope still springs eternal that Rob Lowe will turn up on the other team's softball crew. So far, no luck in that department. But, again, the games and postwin pub crawls are a great way to unwind after work.

Yet another good mix of fun and fitness is the local dance studio. Did you take ballet in grade school? You can pick it up again at your local "Y." In addition to helping to burn off those business lunches, your dance training can help improve the posture that will help you stand tall the next time you're presenting your quarterly progress report to your boss.

In some cities, you can work out with professional dancers as well, taking classes at their training schools. In Philadelphia, for example, the Waves dance company opens some of its sessions to outsiders. If you're a true dance fan, and are advanced enough to keep up, you can star-gaze and strengthen your muscles at the same time.

The list of options goes on and on, with sporting opportunities to suit every temperament and budget. If you live in a warm climate, head for the community tennis or golf courses. (Often, those run by the municipality are free—or far cheaper than private playing grounds.) Where it's colder, you can play basketball at the local gym in the snow season, or touch football in the park when the leaves fall. If you like to exercise, you should have no trouble finding where to do so.

But what if you don't? What if your idea of weight lifting (like mine) is carrying the groceries home, and the only time you put on a bathing suit is to even out your tan? According to the medical experts, you really should force yourself, anyway. The medical recommendation is to get your heart really pumping for forty-five minutes at least three times a week. Palpitations from watching "Charlie's Angels" reruns or Paul Newman movies do not count. If you can't stand the thought of donning a neon leotard and dancing to disco music in an overheated room with mirrors around its perimeter, invest in an audio-cassette and do Jane Fonda at home. Or, if you have a VCR, get the video tape and watch a woman twice your age put you to shame. Guilt and envy have been known to be wonderful motivators. . . .

When I lived in London for a semester, my friend Jill and I "made it burn" to the tone of Jane's voice on our dual-voltage cassette player every night. Despite my diet of Cadbury bars and fried fish, I lost fifteen pounds that semester. Ever since, I'm unable to watch late-night reruns of *Barbarella* or *On Golden Pond* without getting charley horsed.

I've never been able to maintain that level of daily dedication since I lost my exercise partner. But who knows—maybe now that I've publicly shamed myself by admitting this I'll start again.

If you'd like someone who, unlike Jane Fonda, doesn't play the same songs each time you rewind the tape, you can (finances permitting) have an exercise pro come to your home. What an age we live in! You can't get a house call for a *broken* leg, but for fat ones, help is just a phone call away. Look in the classified section of your city magazine, and make some phone calls. Get lots of references before you have this muscle-building Mohammed come to your mountain; quacks abound. But like the girl with the curl, when personal trainers are good, they're very, very good. No matter how you choose to exercise, "the hardest thing is starting," says my friend Betsy. "I have a tough time forcing myself to go to dance class, but once I do, I feel great. It really helps me relax."

If your muscles are sore from jumping too quickly from the wimp class to advanced aerobics, or simply from stress, you may want to spend the money for a professional massage periodically. Better yet, find a willing volunteer. A cute, willing volunteer. He/she will not only dekink your muscles, but maybe (maybe?!) distract you from the budget analysis you left at the office or the fight you had with your father.

28

In the Long Run

Avoiding the Side Effects of Stress

For most of us, there's really no way to eliminate stress totally from our lives. Depending on your personality, this stress can be a source of motivation or a font of long-term health trouble.

Jeff Davidson, author of *Breathing Space* (MasterMedia), offers the following tips for breaking what he calls the "too busy syndrome":

- Look for activities you can safely drop, such as reading that you think you have to keep up with or always watching the news at 11:00 P.M.
- Schedule visits to friends, physical workouts, and time for hobbies, just as you schedule career-related activities. Then stick to the schedule.
- Linger a few moments before going from one activity

to the next. There is no rush, except for the one you help to create.

- Handle your errands on week nights—not on weekends.
- Schedule a weekend vacation and then cancel it. You'll have a whole weekend to do whatever you want—hike, visit friends, or write poetry.
- Use all reasonably priced services that will relieve you of errands/repairs/shopping.
- Make having greater peace of mind a goal, just as you have career, income, and relationship goals.
- Ask your employer if you can telecommute at least once a week. Stay in touch by phone, fax, and modem.
- Cancel subscriptions that you can't keep up with anyway. Then go to the library and review issues every couple of months.
- Actively support only a handful of causes, instead of giving intellectual energy to dozens.
- Go a whole weekend without listening, reading, or talking about the news.
- Eliminate 70 percent of your junk mail. Write to:
  Direct Marketing Association
  11 West 42nd Street
  P.O. Box 3861
  New York, NY 10163-3861
  and ask to be included on their "doesn't want junk mail" list.
- Note: The average person spends a total of eight full months of his/her life reading junk mail!
- Get to bed by 9:00 P.M. one evening per week. You'll feel like a new person in the morning.

Much has been said about the "type A" personality. The stereotypical workaholic that we picture as a little overweight and a lot overstressed has been the subject of countless books, articles, and doctors' warnings. If you *are* driven to the point where it might eventually endanger your heart, be doubly sure to follow these risk-reducing tips from the American Heart Association:

- Keep your weight down.
- Quit smoking.
- Have your cholesterol checked and, if it's high, change your diet.
- Get enough exercise.

Besides heart disease, another prevalent form of stress-related illness, Dr. Kirk Zachary says, is stomach trouble. He's right. Just ask *me*. While I'm not likely to suffer heart failure if I fail to double my department's quarterly profits, a broken heart always makes me sick to my stomach. In college, my friends and I called it "new boyfriend disease," that queasy run-to-the-john feeling that you're never sure is love or botulism. Nervous stomach, or "irritable bowel syndrome," as this condition is technically called, can strike when you're stressed at work or at home, or when you're nervous about an upcoming event. The symptoms can be treated with smooth-muscle-relaxing drugs (ask your physician about these). But before you try medication, try alleviating your symptoms by modifying your diet. There is scientific evidence that a high-fiber diet can minimize the symptoms of irritable bowel syndrome.

Ulcers are another common form of stress-related illness. Once the scourge of middle-aged men, this painful condition has crossed age and gender lines. If you suspect an ulcer (a week of that cheap-Mexican-food feeling is a tip-off, as I learned), see your doctor. He or she will diagnose you with either a "GI" series (so-called either because it stands for gastrointestinal, or because, like war, it is hell) or an endoscopic test that involves your swallowing a tube the diameter of a frankfurter and feeling it go down fifteen feet of intestine. These tests are unpleasant, but an untreated ulcer can spell trouble, big time.

Stress can also cause several less threatening symptoms: sleeplessness, fatigue, and acne. The first two can be treated by getting to the root of the problem or drinking warm milk. The last improves when you avoid fatty foods, keep your hands away from your face, and ask your dermatologist what he recommends to clear up breakouts.

29

Sound of Mind

Dealing with Real Life

Exercise, massage, and medical care can help you deal with the physical by-products of stress, but it's also important to distract your mind, so that you can forget, or at least minimize, the small, everyday annoyances that can leave you with an Excedrin headache. Everyone I interviewed had his own remedy for stress. These ranged from the ambitious: "I go into my studio and paint"; to the productive: "I clean out my closets"; to the less-than-recommended: "I get really, really drunk."

If you're finding that this last plan of action is becoming a more frequent solution to your problems, you may be developing another, more serious problem. If you suspect you're developing a drinking or drug problem, quit NOW. If you're already in too deep to quit on your own, get help. Look in the back of your phone book for the alcohol or drug abuse hotline, and use that number.

Sometimes, it's helpful just to discuss your stresses with a friend or roommate, and to realize that your friends are all going through the same things you are. When that's not sufficient, a psychologist or counselor might be helpful.

Clinical psychologist Cheryl Fishbein says you should seek professional psychological help immediately if you've given even a fleeting thought to suicide. Call a local hotline as a stopgap measure, but even when the feeling has passed, you should talk with someone who can help you figure out what's bothering you and how to deal with it.

Other signs that you need help are a feeling that you have no options or that things are bleak and not going to get better. If you've lost or gained a lot of weight without consciously trying, you may be more depressed than you realize (or you may be sick; if you feel okay emotionally, get a checkup).

On a less drastic basis, you may want to see a psychologist or social worker if you're having trouble adjusting to your new life, or if you feel you're unable to leave college behind you and start your new life with a reasonable amount of confidence and good cheer.

Or you may want to seek help when you're overwhelmed by that first inevitable setback. We all face failure from time to time; the trick is learning how to deal with it constructively.

30

The Road to Recovery

What to Do If You've Lost Your Job—or Your Balance

"It was the scariest thing to happen to me—certainly since I graduated, but probably in my life. It only lasted a short while, but it seemed like forever. I was all alone, and I didn't know what would happen to me if it got worse. I began to think it was never going to stop."

Brad Schooler's description of the Los Angeles earthquake in 1987 could easily describe the feelings other recent graduates have had during their own "worst moments." Everyone I questioned has survived at least one truly awful experience since graduation, and some have had more than their fair share. What's heartening is that everyone seems to come through, sometimes with a greater sense of confidence or with the realization that what seemed like a tragedy at one time was, in retrospect, "the best thing that ever happened to me."

In October of 1986, I faced a job shake-up that absolutely blew my confidence. Despite the excellent job my boss and I and nine of the ten members of our client's team thought I was doing, the tenth man, who had the most power, took a dislike to me. I was out. Period. No arguments from me, my boss, or her boss could change the verdict. The fact that I had gotten more publicity for the client than anyone had promised them was beside the point, as was the fact that the client's communications officer with whom I had the most contact thought the world of me. Bottom line: the client dumped me.

For a week, I walked around in a daze. I would leave the country, I thought—maybe pick oranges on a kibbutz. I would sue the offender for defamation of character. I would never talk to or trust anyone again. I would certainly quit my job.

"I don't think you should quit," my boss said. "Everyone here knows you're doing a good job, and your career isn't going to suffer. But if you *are* going to quit, maybe you should talk to Susan Stautberg [a friend of my boss's, whom I had met previously]. She knows about all the fields you're interested in; maybe she can give you some ideas."

By the time Susan and I could arrange a meeting, I had been given a new assignment at my agency, and had already decided that the change was a positive one. Still, I went to chat with her, hoping to find out about free-lance writing opportunities. We talked about what I wanted to do—which was write. We talked about what she does, which is publish. After a few more conversations with Ms. Stautberg, the president of MasterMedia, I had an even stronger belief that my so-called disaster really wasn't so bad after all. And I had something better: a commitment to publish this book.

Now, not every obstacle I've encountered has led to a

book contract. But at the risk of sounding like a Pollyanna, I can honestly say that most have turned out for the best. A guy I was dating dumped me right before I was going to ask to interview his sister, a nutritionist. So I found another nutritionist. And after Gail Levey gave me her bran muffin recipe, she gave me her apartment, cheap. Real cheap.

Of course, there are some real tragedies that lead to nothing but grief. My grandmother died about a year after I graduated; both of my grandfathers have passed away since then. It's hard for me to think about it (or write about it) without crying. Even now.

Many of the people I've interviewed have lost loved ones as well, or experienced similar tragedies. The older we get, the more frequently this happens. The only consolation is that this is part of the cycle of life.

And, frankly, so are the more minor calamities we encounter. In the introduction to *Real Life 101*, I stated that you can't consider yourself a graduate of this intro course until you have learned some really hard lessons. The first of these is that everyone screws up sometimes. The chairman of your company, I promise you, has made plenty of mistakes. So have your parents, your boss, and the president of your senior class.

Soon after I graduated, I met a woman whose life seemed unjustly easy. Liane was successful, well liked, newly married and deliriously happy with her husband. I would have bet that the worst thing ever to happen to *her* was a broken nail. I would have lost. I would have given my soul to trade places with her. I would have *really* lost, on that one.

Between the time she graduated in the early seventies and my own entrance into Real Life, she had been through six jobs, a short-lived, previous marriage, and hundreds of tearstained diary pages.

"I was fired from my first job," she says. "I had been

working for a biweekly newsletter that suddenly doubled its frequency—and its subscription rate. A lot of our readers, who were on tight budgets, had to cancel their subscriptions. Because I had been the last one hired, I was the first to go when money got tough. That was hard enough. But my boss really drove the nail in when she told me that I wasn't particularly good at the writing and editing that had been my responsibilities. Not only did I lose my job, then, but my confidence was really shot. I was panicked that I wouldn't find a job, and that my career was totally ruined. From March till October, I looked for a job. Finally, I found work with a government agency, where I worked for three years. But when the government decided to investigate the agency for some suspected wrongdoing, they found out that I had been switched from a temporary worker to a permanent employee in a manner that didn't comply with civil service regulations, and I lost my job."

After a brief stint at another job, she moved to New York and joined the staff of a public relations agency—from which she was let go after a few months. "My style just didn't match with theirs," she says. "But this time, I knew enough to know that I could and would find another job." Sure enough, she did—as a temporary, free-lance worker. When the project she was assigned to reached its natural conclusion, she moved to the agency she's been at for twelve years. There, she has succeeded and become one of the most respected members of the staff. The confidence she has acquired makes it easy for an innocent bystander to assume, as I did, that she'd had smooth sailing all the way up.

"Most people wouldn't tell you about all their disasters," she said after recounting her bumpy job history. "It's part of their professional aura to look as if they have everything under control. But, believe me, every successful person you see has had problems."

Unfortunately, these days it's more likely than ever for young professionals to experience this kind of setback—and even get fired. Over 3 million white-collar workers lost their jobs in 1990, and the number keeps rising—along with the percentage of that number who are being fired from once-safe entry-level positions.

If you do get the axe, you can expect to spend some time feeling angry, bereft, and distressed. According to Emily Koltnow, author of *Congratulations! You've Been Fired,* "When you lose your job, it's perfectly normal to have bouts of depression mixed with anxiety, anger, or fear. We all go through it; after all, you've just experienced a major loss. As long as it doesn't go on too long, give yourself permission to accept the feeling."

To keep it from "going on too long," take an active role in your readjustment. Here are some steps Koltnow suggests taking immediately upon learning you've been terminated:

- Register for unemployment. You've earned it (literally: it's been coming out of your taxes), and unless you're independently wealthy, you're going to need it.
- Get yourself a business card. Having a card with your name, address, and phone number is a big help when you're networking.
- Get a library card. The library has lots of information about job hunting in general and companies in particular. Besides saving money, doing your research in the library rather than buying the books will keep you from sitting around the house all day watching talk shows.

- Since you'll have to put this position on your résumé to account for what you've been doing since graduation, get your termination story straight. What are you going to tell prospective employees when they ask why you're out of work? Will your former employer back this up?
- Check up on your reference. Have a friend pretend to be a prospective employer and call your old boss for a reference. You'll find out soon enough what kinds of things she's saying about you, and will be able to tip interviewers off to the fact that you and your boss parted ways because of a personality conflict or a difference in approach to the job.
- Update your résumé, and make sure it looks perfectly professional.
- Make sure your COBRA (Consolidated Omnibus Reconciliation Act) is in place. By law, your company must allow you to purchase your health plan from them for eighteen months after termination, at their cost. This is usually much cheaper than getting your own insurance.
- Locate helpful organizations. Check the *Directory of Associations* for the names and addresses of organizations related to your field (or the field you might want to switch into). Write for information and take advantage of any networking opportunities these leads turn up for you.

If you can keep yourself organized—and optimistic—a firing will usually turn out for the best. "Be glad your first firing is happening early in your career," says Emily Koltnow. "You'll learn *now* that you can overcome this kind of a setback."

Whatever the setbacks are—to you, your career, or the economy—rest assured they are temporary. Like the phoenix (and like the stock market since October of 1987), careers have a way of rising from their own ashes to soar again—and so does the human spirit. While these are stressful times to be alive, they're also incredibly exciting. The world is changing, and each of us has an opportunity to participate in that change and to mold the future of the planet—as well as our own futures. So if things are tough, remember that it's times like this when the tough truly get going. When you look at the events in your life with some perspective, you'll probably agree with the plurality of my respondents. Almost everyone who sent questionnaires back indicated that they've learned to take things as they come and value what's really important: their family, their friends, and their health. You'll learn that when a door closes, a window opens. Opportunity and enchantment will turn up in the least expected places. If that sounds like something your parents would say, there's a reason: like your folks, the people who answered the questionnaires are GROWNUPS. And most of them are enjoying it. One man even wrote, "Work is better than school."

So hold on to your graduation caps and face the sun. Real Life, here you come!

About the Author

SUSAN KLEINMAN graduated from the University of Pennsylvania in 1986 and has worked in public relations and publishing in New York City for the past six years. Now a free-lance magazine journalist and speechwriter, Ms. Kleinman is co-author of *Managing Your Child's Diabetes* and *Don't Give Up on New York.*

Additional copies of *Real Life 101* may be ordered by sending a check for $9.95 (please add the following for postage and handling: $2.00 for the first copy, $1.00 for each added copy) to:

MasterMedia Limited
17 East 89th Street
New York, NY 10128
(212) 260-5600
(800) 334-8232
(212) 348-2020 (fax)

Susan Kleinman is available for speeches and workshops. Please contact MasterMedia's Speakers' Bureau for availability and fee arrangements. Call Tony Colao at (908) 359-1612.